CENTRE FOR PENTECOSTAL THEOLOGY
NATIVE NORTH AMERICAN CONTEXTUAL
MOVEMENT SERIES

Consulting Editor
Corky Alexander

In *Dreamcatching*, Sue Martell, along with her husband Ray, have crafted a narrative rendition of the life and vision of the late Dr Richard Twiss (Sicangu Lakota), former president of Wiconi, International. Using his unpublished writings, sermons, and journal articles, they 'tune' his history using 'chords' taken from his words to prepare contemporary readers to grasp Richard's vision and legacy and to follow in his footsteps.

First, the authors examine several of Twiss's deeply personal spiritual experiences of faith as a Christ-follower, while giving account of his cultural practices as a Lakota person. Called as a minister of the gospel (trained in the Western-style of evangelicalism), Richard's ultimate transformation, as the Martells conclude, came only through reconciling his own Native American identity with the Scriptures, and taking both seriously. Thereafter, his prophetic voice promoted the use of contextual ministry as a more effective means to bring about the reconciliation of all peoples through Christ. His teaching became widely recognized by evangelicals of all cultures. The result? Richard framed a uniquely Native American contextualization of Christianity that gave meaning, hope, and presence for all nations to do the same.

Second, the Martells awaken today's audiences – those who now see just how essential it is to be multicultural interpreters of Christ's message – so that all may focus on the central truths of the gospel, and then each act by 'dreaming' the right way to follow God into indigenous ministry. Sue narrates her own and her husband's experiences of obeying a vision from God, which led to discovering their call to serve as volunteers for the Wiconi ministry alongside Richard and Katherine Twiss.

The Martells include chapters that give examples of how traditional cultures have intersected with Christian spirituality to enable people to believe in Jesus. This book holds to high biblical guidelines for indigenous and non-indigenous congregations alike. The authors' practical examples of Native traditions, discussion questions, and observations direct readers as to how to behave and belong as outsiders yet participant-observers in the midst of indigenous people, believing in Christ as Creator as well as Savior.

Richard Twiss emerged as a Native American contextual theologian who reached his people – and yet his ideas went beyond them to everyone else. Thus, he proclaimed that all people groups be who God made them to be and follow the gospel of Jesus within their own cultures. Such a message is successfully delivered and illustrated through *Dreamcatching*.

– Dr Eunice L. Irwin, Associate Professor of Mission and Contextual Theology (retired) Asbury Theological Seminary, Wilmore, Kentucky.

DREAMCATCHING

FOLLOWING IN THE FOOTSTEPS OF RICHARD TWISS

DREAMCATCHING
FOLLOWING IN THE FOOTSTEPS OF RICHARD TWISS

SUE MARTELL WITH RAY MARTELL
RICHARD TWISS

Cherohala Press
Cleveland, Tennessee

Dreamcatching: Following in the Footsteps of Richard Twiss
Centre for Pentecostal Theology Native North American Contextual Movement
Series

Published by Cherohala Press
900 Walker ST NE
Cleveland, TN 37311
USA
email: cptpress@pentecostaltheology.org
website: www.cptpress.com

Library of Congress Control Number: 2017958092

ISBN-10: 1935931679
ISBN-13: 9781935931676

The New International Version of the Bible was used unless stated otherwise.
Text by Dr Richard Twiss (Sicangu Lakota) used with permission from Katherine
Twiss.

Dr Casey Church (Potawatomi) assisted as cultural advisor.

Cover design by Kellie Komorita-Martell using original artwork by Sue Martell

Available at special quantity discounts when purchased in bulk by bookstores, organizations, and special-interest groups. For more information, please e-mail
cptpress@pentecostaltheology.org.

Dedication

We owe what we are to those who have gone before us,
and so we dedicate this book to our parents,
Jim and Doris, Harvey and Bernadette,
and the long line of faithful generations before them.
We also wish to honor our children,
Daniel and Jenny,
and the generations who will follow.

CONTENTS

Foreword...xi

Acknowledgments...xv

Introduction...1

PART 1
Following God's Dream for Your Life

Chapter 1
The Beginning of Our Dream: Called into Native American
Ministry...5

Chapter 2
What Do You Do When It Looks Like Your Dream
Has Died?...19

Chapter 3
The Dream of Richard and Katherine Twiss................................23

Chapter 4
The Founding of Wiconi International...45

Chapter 5
Now What? Our Entry into Publishing..55

PART 2
Passing the Torch of Native American Contextual
Ministry to the Next Generation

Chapter 6
Was Everything We were Ever Taught about Native
American Culture and Ministry Wrong? 71

Chapter 7
Navigating Native Culture as a Continuing Learning Process.......81

Afterword
My Name is Written on the Palms of His Hands............................95

Appendix A
God's Purpose for Native People, by Richard Twiss....................97

Appendix B
The Blessing of Covenant: Native Americans and the
Church, by Richard Twiss..99

Appendix C
The Need for Various Styles of Ministry, by Richard Twiss....... 102

Appendix D
The Need for Like-minded Friends, by Richard Twiss 104

Appendix E
Journey to Israel, A Diary, by Richard Twiss 106

Following Creator's Son Jesus.. 115

Bibliography... 116
Index of Biblical References... 118
Index of Names... 119
About the Authors... 120
Ministry Resources... 121

FOREWORD

My friends Ray and Sue Martell edited the late Dr Richard Twiss's book, *Rescuing the Gospel from the Cowboys: A Native American Expression of the Jesus Way*. They entered the world of contextual ministry much later than most of us, but soon became valuable partners to the Wiconi ministry as the editors of my doctoral dissertation and my book *Holy Smoke: The Contextual use of Native American Ritual and Ceremony*.

Their dream to serve Native Americans in ministry began by volunteering at area cultural events, sharing life with contextual partners, and studying the cultural traditions of many Native American tribes. The more involved they became, the more they found out just how much they needed to know about the Native American world in order to find their place in it. The doors to working with Richard Twiss and Wiconi soon opened wide and they began serving as volunteers at Wiconi Family Camp. Later, they partnered with Richard as editors, converting his doctoral dissertation into a book which would eventually be published by InterVarsity Press. Before this project was to come to completion, tragedy struck and Richard passed from this world to the next.

There was much left undone. Richard knew that for the gospel to be meaningful to Native American people, it must be filtered through and expressed within the cultural language and context of the people. At Katherine Twiss's request, Ray and Sue were now faced with the challenge of finishing the book without Richard's presence, yet it *was* published and has become a foundational text describing the history of the Native American Contextual Ministry Movement.

As an added blessing, left behind were bins of his letters, notes, and sermons. They were to become the basis for this book, and are included as excerpts showing Richard's journey from Western-style evangelical pastor to contextual practitioner. Using these sources full of memories and messages, the Martells would once again embark on a 'mission impossible' project. Their dream of ministry to Native Americans began when they worked with Richard on *Rescuing the Gospel from the Cowboys,* and now the dream continues through the creation of this book. These previously lost but now compiled memories give us an unexpected glimpse into the founding of Wiconi International.

The Martells' journey has offered them a greater knowledge of the Native American world and has also caused them to grow in their faith. One of their strongest desires in editing *Rescuing the Gospel from the Cowboys,* and writing and editing this book, is the 'passing of the torch' of contextual ministry to the next generation, and to teach the adults as well.

It doesn't often happen that thoughts, ponderings, and imagination all come together in the same book. This is the story of two journeys: Ray and Sue's, and Richard and Katherine's. Every word in this dual story stems from a passionate desire to serve the Lord Jesus Christ.

Richard's words give much food for thought to those who may question the use of contextualization. It is birthed in the Scriptures and useful for service in contemporary Native American culture. Richard lived life at the academic grass-roots level. He recognized the long overdue need to put unfruitful ministry approaches behind us and accept a contextual style to be used alongside older methods.

The work Ray and Sue Martell have done has rendered all of us a service. They tackled the stacks of notes, letters, and sermons to give us a glimpse into Richard's early journey into contextualization. These preserved words come to us years after Richard's passing, and are insights into his genius. His words flowed from his heart and soul so naturally through his pen. There is a great need to increase the body of literature useful for training contextual practitioners. This book is a welcome addition, and will be used in that way.

I believe *Dreamcatching: Following in the Footsteps of Richard Twiss* will become standard reading for those interested in understanding their individualized formative spiritual journeys. May this book be a token of our deep appreciation for who you are and what the Lord has in store for you.

Ray and Sue have helped us come to terms with Richard Twiss' cultural yet transcultural view of the Holy Scriptures, so we can apply it to our own personal journeys toward intercultural ministry, that is, 'Contextual Ministry'.

Well done my friends!

Dr Casey Church
(Potawatomi), Intercultural Studies, Adjunct Professor for Fuller Theological Seminary, Director of Wiconi, and author of *Holy Smoke: The Contextual Use of Native American Ritual and Ceremony.*

ACKNOWLEDGMENTS

The Lord called Abraham to leave all that was familiar and follow him into uncharted territory. We are eternally grateful to our Creator for calling us to follow him into – what were for us – the 'uncharted places' of service to Native American people.

We have benefitted from the prayers of our families, ministry co-workers, brothers and sisters at Wiconi and NAIITS: An Indigenous Learning Community, Dr. Lou LaBombard (Seneca), and many other Native friends we have been blessed with locally. *We extend our thanks to all of them.*

We are indebted to Dr Casey Church (*Ankwawango*/Hole in the Clouds), Director of Wiconi, for acting as cultural advisor. *We appreciate his wisdom and guidance.*

And, *Dreamcatching* would not even exist but for Katherine Twiss' extraordinary generosity. Thanks *so much* for your friendship and for allowing us to include excerpts of Richard's unpublished sermons and letters in this book.

In Richard's memory, we would like to extend a special blessing to his mother, Winona Larvie LaPointe, a godly woman who faithfully prayed over his life and ministry.

INTRODUCTION

The word of the LORD came to me, saying, 'Before I formed you in the womb I knew you, before you were born I set you apart; I appointed you as a prophet to the nations' (Jer. 1.4-5).

Is there more? Is there more of God for us? If God is infinite – and he is – the answer is 'Yes'.

God in his generosity gave us all free will. God said he knew Jeremiah before he was born. He was called as a prophet to the nations; but Jeremiah, having free will, could have chosen to live a 'normal' life as perhaps a tentmaker, shepherd – or maybe even a baker! But, he chose to follow God's best plan for his life and impacted generations for millennia as a result.

I believe we all have a similar choice available to us. We can, as believers, choose to follow our own path – even into acceptable and needed professions – and not *truly* be walking in God's best plan for us. We would still spend eternity with Christ, but not, as I believe, living to the fullest expectation or possibility in God while here on earth.

It really is all about choice – our choices. Your best plan from God doesn't always come to fruition immediately upon deciding to ask for it, but it does begin the process – the journey. After years of directing my own path – while a believer – I resolved to allow God full control over every aspect of my life and every 'corner' of my heart. I believe that all of us can and should ask for as much of the Lord as we can get. Some will have a 'quiet ride', some a 'wild' and more public one. All types of callings are equally important to the bringing in of the Kingdom of God.

My husband Ray and I embarked on the journey to our destined purpose in God when our calling to serve Native and Indigenous people was confirmed in 2007. The late Dr Richard (Sicangu Lakota) and Katherine Twiss were called into their destiny – Native American contextual ministry – in 1975. Our paths intersected with theirs in 2009.

Part 1 of this book tells our separate and then mutual stories until and beyond Richard's unexpected passing in February 2013.

Part 2 is written to share something of what we as cultural outsiders have learned in order to help those called into cross-cultural service, as we have been.

It is our greatest wish – our prayer – that Jesus-followers from all cultural backgrounds seek and then choose God's best plan for them.

May we choose to join the ranks of those who 'turned the world upside down' (Acts 17.6, NKJV). We are indeed those '*called according to His purpose*' (Rom. 8.28).

PART 1

Following God's Dream for Your Life

Then I heard the voice of the Lord saying,
'Whom shall I send? And who will go for us?'

And I said, 'Here am I. Send me!' (Isa. 6.8)

1

THE BEGINNING OF OUR DREAM: CALLED INTO NATIVE AMERICAN MINISTRY

Weavings of Remembrances

I close my eyes and I am there still. I return to the swirling fragrance of dust, parched grass, cedar, and burning sage. The heat of the sun is wrapped around me like a thick, comforting blanket. I am electrified by the rhythmic heartbeat of the drums, travelling to the depths of my soul and spreading across the powwow grounds – so intense I can feel the ground tremble through the soles of my bare feet. In and out I breathe the prayer-drenched atmosphere.

Prayers have been offered to bless the occasion – not just in English, but also the original languages of this land.

Veterans carrying the Stars and Stripes, the military service flags, and an eagle staff – the flag of the original peoples – march around the outside of the arena with more veterans and dancers trailing behind.

There are my new friends with long hair woven into braids, dressed in wildly-bright regalia embellished with eyesight-defying beaded treasures. Jingle bells on moccasins imitate thunder.

Children with smiling eyes chase each other, weaving in and out among their families, trailing glossy black hair and the multi-hued feathers and ribbons of their regalia. The children are beautiful.

Vendors and their artwork are protected from the sun by one gazebo after another. Old friends visit back and forth. Stories are etched on the faces of the elders.

The musical styles are unexpected and compelling to me. Dancers float and swirl; puffs of dust rise around their acrobatic feet.

I am enfolded by community and accepted with great grace. There is an unquestionable sense of knowing that the hand of God has put us (Ray and me) here as a piece of a much larger puzzle. There is a deep, thick sense of the presence of God and a realization that I have been placed in the center of my destiny – precisely where I belong.

I should not have been comfortable here – but I have never been so comfortable anywhere. The truth is I always felt like 'the odd one out' among my Christian brothers and sisters – like I really didn't belong – like I hadn't found my place and purpose in Creator's story.

Today I knew beyond the core of my being that I was finally 'home'.

Our Journey Begins

As I look back on it now, our journey into Native American ministry began before we even realized it. Ray and I talk from time to time about events from our past. Even our childhood memories show evidence of God's hand on our lives deliberately (and sometimes blatantly) directing us to this place at the Wiconi Family Camp and Pow-wow in Turner, Oregon.

Ray and I met in 1982 while in the Air Force. I was a nurse and he was a missile officer. We married later that year, and after seven months I got a transfer from Ohio to Arizona where Ray was stationed. Over the years, we travelled around the world and then started our family first with a son in Portugal and then a daughter in England.

I chose to resign my commission in order to be at home with our children. Ray served in Operation Desert Storm on General Schwarzkopf's staff as a media relations officer. It was terrifying watching the live TV news and seeing SCUD missiles heading directly to where I believed my husband to be.

We were blessed that the war was short and Ray was home soon.

While stationed in Washington State in 1995, Ray and I decided to take a cruise to Alaska. Although raised as Christians, neither of us was really walking with the Lord at the time.

My Dad's family is mostly United Presbyterian (UP), and that is how I was raised. My mom's family is Catholic, although by marriage we can cover many Christian denominations. I met Jesus as a nine-year-old in a United Presbyterian Church Vacation Bible School. My parents became born again about a year later. Three years after that the Charismatic renewal was in full-swing, and my parents became friends with several of the people involved. Soon all of us received the baptism of the Holy Spirit. I was active in that movement from then until I was a young adult. After joining the Air Force, I still believed in Jesus, but money and career became my gods. That's the way it was when we went on our cruise.

One of the Alaska cruise destinations was the quaint, picturesque, seaside town of Sitka. We took a bus tour of the area and one of the stops was St. Michael's Cathedral. I was particularly interested in their icon collection because I am also a watercolor artist. When our tour group entered the church, we were met by a gentleman who described himself as a Tlingit (a Native Alaskan tribe) brother in the Russian Orthodox Church. He offered to lead us in the Lord's Prayer in his language. As he prayed the power of God became tangible in the place. It was as if there were a powerful cloud of the glory of God in the church. The brother then gave us a brief history of St. Michael's. He emphasized that the icon of Mary (Our Lady of Sitka) was noted for miraculous intervention.

Good Presbyterians do not believe in such things, but at that time in my life my heart was in a desperate place. As we toured the cathedral, I stopped to gaze at the beautiful icon of Mary and felt led to pray that God help my family. When I looked up after that brief prayer I saw Mary standing in front of me. She was a small woman with intense dark eyes. She was wearing a blue shawl and a dress of coarse home-made cloth. She did not speak audibly, but I sensed that she was saying, 'Everything will be alright'.

The next thing I knew, Ray was shaking me, telling me that the bus was leaving. To say that I was stunned would be an understatement. Since good Presbyterians do not have visions of Mary, at the time I only told Ray, my Mom, and his Mom. And since this did not work with my theology, I 'suppressed' the experience for twelve years. I will say that this was a turning point on our walk back to faith.

In September of 2007, exactly twelve years later, we were in Sitka again. This time we went on a cruise there as part of a family reunion in memory of Ray's Dad, who had served in the Merchant Marines as a ship's chief engineer during WW2.

I was a little – ok, a *lot* nervous about a return trip to St. Michael's Cathedral. This time the church priest was there. He was an Alaska Native, as was most of the congregation. He did not say anything to our tour group as a whole, but answered questions the tourists were asking him.

I knew in my heart that God wanted me to tell the priest about my experience twelve years prior, but I was arguing with him about it. I thought the priest would think I was crazy, or that he would just be polite. Then it occurred to me that I would probably never see the man again, so what difference would it make if I told him or not? In the meantime, he had people talking to him already, so I thought I was off the hook. When I turned around, he was alone, so I gave in and went over and told him my story.

I was shocked by his response. He obviously believed what I told him. When I finished, he told me that for the past few months God had been telling him that someone would be coming, and that he was to give his last blessed icon to that person.

He insisted that I not leave until he got the icon for me from his Bible on the altar. He said he was sure it was me that God had told him about, so I accepted the icon. It is now framed and on the wall in our house. It is my most prized possession.

Wow.

Divine Connections

We began to suspect that God was calling us to serve Native people. About two weeks after our time in Sitka, I spent some time in prayer and asked God, saying, 'We don't know anything about Native people. If this is really you, please put good books in front of us so we can learn'.

The next day, I was channel-surfing and saw pastor Richard Twiss (Sicangu Lakota) being interviewed on Trinity Broadcasting Network. I missed most of the interview, but saw the trailer with the Wiconi International ministry website and did hear Richard say he had written a book – *One Church, Many Tribes: Following Jesus the Way God Made You*.[1] I had never seen a Native pastor before and believed this to be more than a coincidence. Ray checked the library catalog – he works in the local library system – and they had a copy of the book!

---

[1] Richard Twiss, *One Church, Many Tribes: Following Jesus the Way God Made You* (Ventura, CA: Regal Books, 2000).

After seeing Richard on TBN in September of 2007, we started reading *One Church Many Tribes* and the books mentioned in the endnotes.

We had been reading about and studying Native ministry and culture when, about a year later, Ray began having some health problems that eventually took five surgeries to correct. A couple of my girlfriends waited with me during the lengthy surgeries. One of those ladies was someone I had just met through our church. Her name is 'June'. June and I talked and got to know each other for four hours while in the waiting room during one of Ray's surgeries.

I felt Holy Spirit intended me to tell her the 'Sitka' story and about Wiconi International, Richard and Katherine Twiss's ministry (Ray and I had looked at the website). Afterwards June said, 'I'll have to tell my friend 'Lissa' about you. She has the same passion for Native American ministry'. June told me that she and Lissa had grown up together and had remained best friends ever since. She also told me that Lissa visited her as often as possible. And she told me that her friend taught at Asbury Theological Seminary in Kentucky.

I said I thought that 'that guy' (Richard) had said that he was attending Asbury. June said that she would ask Lissa if she knew Richard next time she talked to her. June also suggested that she and Lissa and I get together for lunch the next time she visited. Just then Ray came out of surgery and that was the end of the conversation. That was in October 2008.

A few months later in early January 2009, I noticed a promotional trailer on TBN that said Richard Twiss would be interviewed again soon. I called June from work and suggested that she watch the interview. June said she had just talked with Lissa and told her about our previous conversation. June said Lissa said to tell me that 'Sue and Ray should go to "Mission Connexion"[2] next week because Richard Twiss would be teaching there. Also, they should volunteer to help at the Wiconi staff retreat near Seattle in March'. You can imagine how surprised we were to find out how closely connected Lissa was to Richard. She was one of his professors!

By another series of miraculous circumstances, Ray and I both got time off work to leave the following week for Mission Connexion

---

[2] Mission Connexion is a mission-mobilizing organization whose conferences attract thousands of people each year. missionconnexion.com.

Northwest in Portland, Oregon. We attended the Native ministry series of workshops, listened to Richard teach, and met him after the workshop. We told him Lissa had sent us. He signed a copy of *One Church, Many Tribes* for us, and that was the end of the conference.

Late that evening at the motel, we checked our phone messages to find one from June saying, 'Sue, call me as soon as you can. It's urgent'. Since it was late and it didn't sound like a life-threatening emergency, I called June the next day on our way back home. She said, 'Sue, you aren't going to believe this, but Lissa just called me and asked me to call you. She said that Richard and a fellow doctoral student, Randy Woodley, are going to be here tomorrow at a beach house working on their dissertations'.[3] Lissa wanted to know if we would be willing to show them around the island, tell them about good restaurants, and so on.

That's how we ended up eating Chinese food with Richard and Randy two days later! And that is when they asked us to send them the rest of our story (our calling) by email since it was late and we had just told them about our God-led connection with Lissa.

We did end up doing volunteer work at the Wiconi staff retreat in March, but it wasn't in Seattle – it was a few miles from our home. I can still see Richard shaking his head after we told him the series of 'coincidences' that brought us all together!

Meeting New Friends at the Wiconi Staff Retreat

On our island, there is a beautiful seaside estate where a local widow, a godly woman, opens part of her home and nearby beach house to Christian groups for retreats.

Our church ladies' group had had retreats there, and I have very fond memories of the art work, the floor-to-ceiling windows offering views of the beach, ships and boats, and wildlife including herons, hawks, and eagles.

The place feels like a gateway into God's creation as soon as you enter the property. You get the sense that the combined prayers of all the groups who have stayed there saturated the atmosphere and remained hovering over the grounds. That is where the Wiconi staff retreat was held and that is where Ray and I met the rest of our Wiconi friends and their spouses.

---

[3] Randy S. Woodley, PhD, Keetoowah descendant; Distinguished Professor of Faith and Culture, Portland Seminary.

We were invited to share dinner there with them Saturday night. I had volunteered to help with the baking needed for the group of about forty people, and coordinated the breads and desserts with one of Richard and Katherine's sons, the chef providing top-notch meals. I pulled out my family recipes and did my best to provide edible blessings.

Ray and I walked in for dinner Saturday evening not knowing what to expect or who would be there. I was nervous about being in the midst of a group of people from another culture we were only beginning to become familiar with. We were greeted by Richard and Katherine. We were pleasantly surprised to see two women we had met in January at Mission Connexion.

Of all the people we did not yet know, Casey Church[4] made the first effort to come and introduce himself to us. He made us feel welcome and he and his wife remain good friends to this day. He also shared his excellent recipe for Southwestern cornbread with chilies – they live in New Mexico.

I remember being disarmed by the sense of humor encouraged among these close friends. Richard made comments about the risk of eating the bean enchiladas. One of the women loudly objected to only having one trash bag in the kitchen saying, 'We're Indians – what you mean there's no bag for recycling?' Very quickly after her comment a bag was produced for that purpose! I knew if they didn't take themselves seriously, we could relax and be ourselves. We were accepted just as we were.

Time for Making a Choice

After prayer and discussion, only a few weeks later, Ray and I submitted our application to become Wiconi volunteers – and the journey began!

There is no question in our minds that the hand of God crossed our paths with Richard Twiss and Randy Woodley. We have been volunteering for Wiconi and then the North American Institute for Indigenous Theological Studies: An Indigenous Learning Community (NAIITS) ever since. Ray says there are no coincidences and quotes

---

[4] Dr Casey Church is the current director of Wiconi and author of *Holy Smoke: The Contextual Use of Native American Ritual and Ceremony* (ed. Ray Martell and Sue Martell; Cleveland, TN: Cherohala Press, 2017).

Einstein saying, 'Coincidence is God's way of remaining anonymous'.[5]

Getting Our Toes Wet!

Ray and I began doing volunteer work for Wiconi in April of 2009 and still do. We have worked with them in a variety of ways. Ray often works at the book and resources tables at Wiconi-led events or conferences, in addition to helping with elders. I have facilitated watercolor workshops and helped as one of the Wiconi Family Camp nurses.

Even as we volunteered for Wiconi, we wondered what the ultimate destination for our calling was. We had sensed that there was something else coming – something that hadn't even occurred to us.

NAIITS Symposium: George Fox Seminary, Newberg, Oregon, June 2010

Ray and I attended our first NAIITS symposium in June 2010. It was a fresh, new experience to be surrounded by students and academics teaching and learning about or devouring 'new' ideas about Native American contextual ministry. Richard defined contextualization as 'The process of framing the gospel message culturally as either a sacred story or a myth of divine proportions so that it makes sense to people "on the ground" where they live every day'.[6] Randy Woodley, Richard Twiss, Terry LeBlanc, Casey Church, and several other of our Wiconi friends were there conducting workshops and/or presenting papers. Afterwards, we would 'break out' into 'talking circles' (Native-style discussion groups).

We knew that the 2010 symposium was a historic gathering. For many years, our friends had worked toward the goal of starting their own school – a school where students could learn how to effectively reach Native American people for Christ.

The agreement between George Fox Seminary in Newberg, Oregon, and NAIITS was sealed both by contract and a Pipe Ceremony for the creation of a program toward earning a Master of Arts in Intercultural Studies:

---

[5]brainyquote.com/quotes/quotes/a/alberteins574924.html, accessed Mar. 27, 2017.

[6] Richard Twiss, *Rescuing the Gospel from the Cowboys: A Native American Expression of the Jesus Way* (Downers Grove, IL: InterVarsity Press, 2015), p. 243.

Responding to the question of NAIITS' purpose in all of this, Richard Twiss, Lakota and Vice-Chairman of the NAIITS Board of Directors observed: 'Our vision for NAIITS has been to see Native men and women journey down the road of a living heart relationship with Jesus Christ in a transformative way – one which does not require the rejection of their God-given social and cultural identity'.[7]

Since then, NAIITS: An Indigenous Learning Community, has expanded its educational programs to include a BA in Community Development from Providence University College; a Master of Theological Studies – Indigenous from Tyndale University College and Seminary; and an MA in Community Development from Acadia Divinity College.

Most of our Native friends, both men and women, had taken the risk and pursued their doctoral degrees, and many of them are now professors in the NAIITS programs. At this point, they have authored many of the theological textbooks and the curricula besides.

Both NAIITS and Wiconi are now under the covering of Indigenous Pathways: 'Indigenous Pathways is the home to a family of ministries that seek, each in their own areas of expertise, to bring a message of health and well-being to the wider Indigenous community'.[8]

Our First Pipe Ceremony

It was a still, sunny day. We all gathered in the rose garden at George Fox Seminary, Newberg, Oregon, on June 12, 2010. A swirling brick pathway wound through the myriad of colors sprinkled over the petals on the rose bushes – the light fragrance of roses hung in the air. There was a table covered with Native-patterned cloth in the center. Objects on the table included contracts and the means of 'sealing the covenant' – a wooden box containing the sections of a Native American pipe.[9]

Those of us who participated first entered the circle from the east, stopping to be symbolically purified by smoke in a Smudging Ceremony. Then during the Pipe Ceremony, smoke was sent to the four directions and then up to the heavens, down to the earth, and then

---

[7] 'Historic Signing @ George Fox University', *naiits.com*, June 2010, accessed Oct. 28, 2016, naiits.com/news/.

[8] *IndigenousPathways*, indigenouspathways.com/aboutIP.html.

[9] Church, *Holy Smoke*, pp. 81-83.

'center', recognizing Holy Spirit within us. The directions acknowledge Father God our Creator as Lord over all directions of creation, including our hearts.[10] The contracts were signed after the pipe was smoked.

As Randy, who was praying using the pipe, prayed toward us, a low breeze swirled among the rose bushes, sending petals in all directions – a blessing provided by our heavenly Father.

Not having experienced such a ceremony before and given the negative teaching about Native spiritual traditions in my past, I questioned Holy Spirit about the 'appropriateness' of such ceremonies in Christian worship. It is true that I trusted our friends – their lives exemplify and model maturity in Christ. Their obvious heart for their people – and all people from other cultures – was illustrated by their kindness, generosity, unselfishness, and willingness to endure fierce criticism.

For years our friends were accused of syncretism (a theological term that carries the idea of mixing religious beliefs together),[11] banned from Christian organizations, 'uninvited' from speaking engagements, and relegated to remaining 'a mission field' – as opposed to healthy, functioning members of the Body of Christ preparing the way of the Lord and being included in the ushering in of the Kingdom of Heaven on earth. We have seen and continue to see people – Native American and those from other people groups – meet Jesus and have their lives transformed because they are spoken to in their own cultural language and their style of worship through contextual ministry.

I have worked in ministry for more than ten years as the Nurse Manager of a Christian prolife pregnancy care clinic. Ray and I live in a multicultural and multiracial community. Over the years I have used what I have learned from Richard Twiss and our other friends in contextual ministry when witnessing to my clients. About 4% of my clients identify as Native American. Many more are Hispanic or Pacific Islanders; the majority of them are Indigenous people.

Taking the time to learn the cultural languages (at least the basics) of these people groups is very much contextual ministry. I have seen women among these groups return to the clinic after having their

---

[10] Church, *Holy Smoke*, pp. 81-83.
[11] Twiss, *Rescuing the Gospel from the Cowboys*, p. 244.

babies born drug and alcohol free, having completed their GEDs, gone to our local community college for AA degrees or certificates, no longer homeless, and best of all – sometimes choosing to follow Jesus.

Seeing such life-changes and healthy babies continues to bring tears to my eyes and joy to my heart. I often think about Richard's words (and those of our other Native friends) when serving my clients and talking with them about Creator's son, Jesus. I can't express the extent of my gratitude for what I have learned from them and seeing lives changed because they persevered and followed Holy Spirit's leading.

There is no 'outline or formula' for Native American contextual ministry. I never, *ever*, want to 'use' contextualization as a tool. Each person is a precious gift from God to the people of this world. We are all different and created for distinct purposes.

Richard mentioned the concept of 'prophetic contextualization' in *Rescuing the Gospel from the Cowboys*.[12] By this he meant we should learn contextual languages for sharing the gospel, but first and foremost we should follow Holy Spirit's leading in each individual situation. There is no manipulation if you are looking to see and do what the Father is doing, as Jesus modeled for us in Jn 5.19.

The Beginning of the Copyediting Journey

We were invited to the Wiconi staff and volunteer barbecue at the Twiss house after Family Camp in 2012. Since Ray has previous experience as a copyeditor, he offered to critique Richard's doctoral dissertation. By then Richard had self-published a version of it, and wanted to prepare the manuscript for eventual professional publication. After Ray sent samples of his critique to Richard, Richard contacted us and asked if we would work with him to transform his dissertation into a book. We believed it to be God's leading and agreed.

Ray had edited military newspapers, had worked as a broadcast journalist, and had experience in speech writing. It took time in prayer and Ray's encouragement for me to agree to become an active partner in copyediting with Richard and him. I hesitated because my writing/copyediting experience up until that time was in tech writing. I had decades of experience writing and updating medical policies,

---

[12] Twiss, *Rescuing the Gospel from the Cowboys*, p. 207.

procedures, and staff and patient educational programs – not editing theological texts!

I couldn't see past the possibility of merely being the typist for this massive project. I do have experience with word processing and 'cutting and pasting' text to achieve a smooth flow of written thought. (I copyedit our clinic newsletter and other publications). At first I let Richard and Ray work together without my input. But during that time frame, Holy Spirit granted me several clear dreams about my involvement in the process; some we shared with Richard. It became apparent that I was to contribute mainly by looking at the 'big picture' – figuring out what went where and best, and rewriting sentences to make them most understandable for both an academic and non-academic readership.

I have since come to recognize that God's hand had been working me toward this goal for some time. My Dad was formerly the Chairman of the Department of Education (and then Registrar) at Grove City College (a Christian college) in Grove City, Pennsylvania, until his retirement. I had been surrounded by theologians for years and was familiar with much of the terminology.

It was delightful studying Richard's style of written communication. He had a way of writing *very long* sentences. He just kept going and going until he arrived at the point he was planning to make. There were several paragraphs which were comprised of just one sentence apiece.

We talked with Richard about whom he saw as the audience for this book – and if it should be one or *two* books. Later in the process, he chose a more academic style – one book, although we knew he eventually wanted to write another book as a 'popular read'. Early discussion of expanding the section – which included interviews with participants during a Sweat Lodge Ceremony into a book of its own – never happened. Richard described this chapter as the 'heart of the [*Cowboys*] book' and we agreed.

We were in close contact with him until we were stunned by the news that he had suffered a major heart attack while attending the activities surrounding the National Prayer Breakfast in Washington, D.C., in February of 2013.

Discussion Questions

1. God speaks to each of us in different ways. How does he speak to you?

2. If God has called you into Native American or cross-cultural ministry, how do you know that is the case?

3. How should you proceed into your calling if he has asked you to do something you are not trained to do – or into something that seems impossible?

2

What Do You Do When It Looks like Your Dream Has Died?

Tragedy Strikes

My husband Ray and I had been working as copyeditors with our friend Richard Twiss (Sicangu Lakota), transforming his doctoral dissertation into a book – which would eventually become *Rescuing the Gospel from the Cowboys: A Native American Expression of the Jesus Way*.[1] We had been friends for four years, but as we worked together on the book our relationship changed. We went from friends to 'brothers' and 'sister'. We were in close communication working on the manuscript from August 2012 until four days before Richard 'passed on' Feb. 9, 2013.

While he was attending events related to the February 2013 National Prayer Breakfast in Washington, D.C., he was stricken by a sudden heart attack. He remained on this earth surrounded by his family and friends in the hospital for a few days and then 'walked on' to heaven.

We were all devastated by his passing. I had never mourned so deeply for anyone other than family. My grief confused me. I couldn't grasp why the death of a friend – even a close friend – had created an earthquake within me.

After an extended season of darkness and 'tremors' in my soul, I came to the realization that the soul-wrenching grief was not just about our friend's death – there was much more to it than that. We

---

[1] Twiss, *Rescuing the Gospel from the Cowboys*.

were also mourning the death of a dream – a promise from God placed in our hearts years earlier.

During our time of searching, Katherine asked us to bring the *Cowboys* book to completion and publication on her behalf. We were honored by her trust in us and the book was published by InterVarsity Press in June 2015.

Ray and I were not the only ones with a dream from God. Richard had a divine encounter and met Jesus on a beach in Maui in 1972.[2] He later described a vision God had given him in 1975:

> I saw myself before great crowds, being a leader of people. I saw myself being used in substantial ways in the Christian Native American community.[3]

Richard pastored a church in Vancouver, Washington, for thirteen years before he and Katherine entered into full-time ministry serving Native American people.

During that time frame (and for the rest of his life) Richard was a prolific writer. In addition to his books, he authored many magazine articles, anthology entries, and gave presentations to a wide variety of organizations. He was interviewed several times on Trinity Broadcasting Network's 'Praise the Lord' program, Focus on the Family's radio broadcast, and was a guest on the 700 Club, among other venues.

And Then There Were the Bins

Katherine had given us the remainder of Richard's writings, including sermons and other manuscripts authored from 1984-2012. They had been placed into two eighteen-gallon plastic bins.

We had no doubt there was enough material to 'birth' another book in those bins containing *stacks and stacks* of documents. We believed that we had been gifted with treasure from above. We had wanted so badly to get to know Richard better for many years to come. In a way, being gifted with his words from the past gave us that opportunity.

---

[2] Richard's incredible testimony is detailed in both of his books: *One Church, Many Tribes* and *Rescuing the Gospel from the Cowboys*.

[3] Richard Twiss, 'Following God's Dream for Your Life' (sermon presented at New Discovery Community Church, Vancouver, WA, Feb. 1993).

Most of the sermons from 1984-1994 were sorted into folders by topics and years – easy to work on, we thought, but only briefly. *Many, many* sermons were loosely stacked on top of the sorted ones – much more work than we had expected.

The task seemed daunting, but very much worth the effort. We knew Richard's anointed words had the potential to bring about the salvation of many. That is what we wanted too – not just a tribute to our dear friend. We knew that is what he would want as well.

We spent time in prayer about how God would have us compile Richard's writings into a new book. God answered and made it clear that this book was to be the story of Richard and Katherine's journey – the story of their God-given dream of reaching Native people for Christ. We were astonished when we realized that God was also saying it was to include the story of our journey – and our God-given dream.

Discussion Questions

1. How do you deal with fear of the unknown?

2. Write about a time when a God-given dream seems to have died.

3. How do you overcome criticism or road blocks on the way to your God-given dream?

3

THE DREAM OF RICHARD AND KATHERINE TWISS

Back to the Past

After transcribing the majority of Richard's sermons, we found 'buried treasure' in folders we had not yet sorted through. They contained many letters of correspondence – multiple 'snail mail' conversations ranging from 1987-2012. We began to see a gradual yet powerful awakening of Native thoughts and ideas coming from the sermons and letters.

But how can you step into someone else's past and tell their story, essentially, to watch their 'home movies'? We started by reading the letters and newspaper clippings, and looking at old pictures we found online. That's where I found an old photo of Richard and Katherine sitting on the grass in Alaska on a sunny afternoon in the 1970s at the Gospel Outreach mission there. You can see 'young love' in their eyes and the anticipation of a happy life together. I came across a photo in a 1992 newspaper clipping containing an interview with Pastor Richard. He had served at New Discovery Community Church (NDCC) in Vancouver, Washington, for ten years by then, and among other things, he talked about the history of our government's past treatment of Native Americans. You could tell there was a growing restlessness and discomfort with his practicing Christianity from the standpoint of another culture.

These yellowed newspaper clippings, photos, and magazine articles offered a rare glimpse, 'a door' into the past. An undertone of grief and nostalgia was present as I tried to put all these fragments together. It was like looking for all the pieces of a puzzle to get a greater picture of the whole.

It made me smile and sit up in my computer chair as I continued down the timeline (truly a paper trail!) and read the names of people Richard and Katherine had just met for the first time in letters from the mid-to-late 1990s. Many of those friends, new to *them* at the time, are now friends of *ours* as well – met later on our mutual journey.

We had wanted – expected – to get to know Richard and Katherine as a couple for many years to come. We grieved not just for our late friend Richard, but also for the life adventures we could have shared in the future. Discovering Richard's letters in addition to his many sermons helped us to know better where our friends had been in the past, and gave us an unexpected insight into their lives at the time. It occurred to us that in a way, Richard's letters could tell his story in his own words.

The letters included in this chapter trace the triumphs, obstacles, and remarkable journey of Richard 'finding himself as a Lakota follower of Jesus', and his passion for his people and their salvation. Richard's Lakota name was *Taoyate Ob Najin*, 'He Stands with His People'. His letters vividly illustrate the reality of the prophetic nature of his name.

Richard's Earlier Years
Richard described his personal testimony of meeting Jesus on a beach in Hawaii in 1972 in both *One Church, Many Tribes* and *Rescuing the Gospel from the Cowboys*. He also outlined his childhood and then his involvement as a teenager in the American Indian Movement's (AIM) takeover of the Bureau of Indian Affairs building in Washington, D.C., in 1972.

After his encounter with Jesus in Hawaii, Richard relocated to the Gospel Outreach communal ministry in Wasilla, Alaska, at the recommendation of a Christian friend who lived there. The 'Jesus Movement' was in full swing at the time. The ministry, under the leadership of Jim Durkin,[1] began in Eureka, California, and spread up the West Coast to Alaska. Gospel Outreach churches were Christian communes and training centers for those disaffected with the Church as it was at the time – not uncommon during the 1960s. The communes

---

[1] goalumni.homestead.com/index.html, Gospel Outreach web page, accessed Nov. 21, 2016.

trained the students how to be future pastors and missionaries, and also how to live in a Christian community. They started businesses such as the 'Bread of Life Bakery' to help support and feed the communities – Richard worked as the head baker. He learned about business and finance – and bread baking! – while working there. That is where Richard met Katherine, and they were married soon after. They would later transition from baking literal bread to offering the 'Bread of Life' to others through ministry.

Nothing is Impossible

I managed a small bakery in Alaska for several years. We had to make enough bread to fill our daily orders. At one point I felt we could not make any more than a certain number of loaves because of our production equipment and staff. I tried and tried but became convinced we could not possibly bake any more loaves per night within the time period we were allowed. Meanwhile my manager was convinced we could. I went on a ten-day vacation during which time my manager ran the daily business. Upon returning I was told the bakery was producing nearly 20% more bread with the same equipment, same number of employees, and in the same time.

Because of my unwillingness to persevere the test and meet the challenge, we never grew. My manager overcame the limitations of past experiences and failures by persevering in his convictions and by refusing to identify with the past. His perseverance produced a new perspective and greater productivity in the business.

In conclusion, I want to state that the believer who will endure the trials, pressures, and temptations in life is the one who perseveres in Christ. Some will trust in horses, others in chariots, and some in the flesh. But all of these have one thing in common: eventual failure. There will be pressure to quit, pressure to give up on this ministry business, pressure to settle for something a little less demanding – requiring less of me.

To persevere in anything other than Christ is short-term, temporal, and insufficient to keep you. Paul said he endured the light momentary afflictions in this life because of a far more exceeding and eternal glory which awaited him. He persevered in Christ. [2]

---

[2] Richard Twiss, (untitled essay for a class assignment, 1987).

Richard described the Gospel Outreach training as 'evangelical,' and you can see evidence of that in his earlier sermons. We found a newspaper clipping among those sermons which included a photograph of Pastor Twiss and his family. Richard looked every bit a conservative evangelical pastor in his black suit and tie! Later he would be quoted as saying:

> In my first fourteen years of embracing Jesus, I conformed to the expectation of accepting interpretations of the Bible that said 'old things had passed away and all things had become white' – regarding my following Jesus in the context of Native ways of music, dance, drumming, ceremony, and culture. This meant I needed to leave my Indian ways behind me because I had a new identity in Christ and it *was not* Indian![3]

Nevertheless, Richard always seemed to have the dream God gave him – propelling him toward his destiny in Christ. He had been granted a dream from God and chose to follow it no matter what – one step at a time.

God's Timing

Today is the acceptable time, for tomorrow never comes. Over the years I have often been approached by believers who wonder how much longer they need to wait or to learn until God can or will use them. Often they compare themselves to someone else, thinking they have to become *them* before God will use them. You will never be more prepared to serve God than you are today.[4]

When Richard and Katherine plunged into ministry, putting 'feet' on their choice to follow God's call, they relocated to Vancouver, Washington. They began their work at the Gospel Outreach Fellowship church (later named New Discovery Community Church/ NDCC) in 1981.

Richard's earliest sermons focused on scriptural topics, heavily researched in the original Greek and Hebrew, and hand-written on yellow notebook paper. Pages of copies from reference books were stapled to the sermons. Also included were notes taken in classes on

---

[3] Twiss, *Rescuing the Gospel from the Cowboys,* p. 82.
[4] Richard Twiss, 'You Will Never Be More Ready to Serve God than You Are Today' (sermon presented at New Discovery Community Church, Vancouver, WA, July 19, 1987).

biblical studies, writing, and public speaking. It was clear that he did much reading and studying in obedience to his calling – indicating that he had taken his decision very seriously. I can picture him up late at night poring over these books and manuscripts.

In the folders from about 1985 on, we began to notice increasing mention of Native American topics and Richard's own background as a Native man. He was obviously keeping his dream from God in the forefront of his mind.

'Forward Edge' and Short-term Missions

In 1987, the letters began with correspondence with the founder of Forward Edge, at the time a short-term mission agency.[5] Richard was very excited about organizing and participating in Forward Edge mission trips to both the Crow reservation in Montana and the Rosebud reservation in South Dakota. It became clear that he was walking toward the fulfillment of his God-given vision of being used in Native American ministry.

An early letter to Forward Edge illustrates this beginning transition:

July 7, 1987

Dear Brother,

Greetings to you and your family in Jesus' name.

I want to simply communicate on a personal level here about my recent visit to the Rosebud Sioux Indian Reservation. It was a life-changing, thought provoking, and challenging experience for me. It caused me to evaluate many, even most of my assumptions and present practices in the realms of *church growth!* To a large measure it pointed out how I had fallen victim to the 'American Dream' of, in religious enterprises, pastoring a large and successful church – in the sense that success is measured by money, numbers, and size. It presently is symptomatic of the 'success mentality' that has affected the church just as profoundly as the mainstream of secular thought.

The present situation for American Indians living on the reservation shattered many of my new-found church growth principles.

---

[5] Forward Edge now works in relief and development. www.forwardedge.org.

They simply are irrelevant and pointless in the context of reservation life. So in light of these startling new personal revelations, I am quitting the ministry and getting a tee-pee and moving somewhere in the heart of the Black Hills, where I can grow close once again to mother earth and the Great Spirit! Just kidding!! Though I am not quitting or moving, I am re-evaluating what and how it is that I am doing the things I do, relative to pastoring a growing church.

I have pondered my Indian heritage for many years, and as a Christian have mostly shelved the issue and postponed any real dealings with it. I still haven't come to any substantial conclusions, but have at least taken it off the shelf. I went back to the reservation completely neutral and open to anything God may bring onto my path.

Anyway, that is a brief report about 'Indian Country and Me'. A new ring is forming in the tree, I suppose.

I look forward to hearing from you.

Your good buddy,

Richard[6]

Native American Ministry Beginnings through Forward Edge

As many of you know, I am of Native American ancestry. This August my family and I will be leading a short-term mission team through Forward Edge Ministry. We will be going back to my reservation in Rosebud, South Dakota.

We'll do construction work, evangelism, and some teaching.

There are many problems among Native American people. Many of you are aware of the alcohol, poverty, suicide, and lack of vision in the Native American community. The reason I have chosen to *wear my hair a little longer* is that culturally – among the younger and more traditional men – it is preferred.

One thing that has disturbed me in ministry among Native people is that the problem is more the Church's past work among Native people than the people themselves. It is something I see in

---

[6] Richard Twiss, letter to the director of Forward Edge, 7 July 1987.

the Church today as well: separation, judgment, comparison, and criticism.

In the Church there are many different views, perspectives, opinions, and ways of thinking. This is the beauty and diversity of the Church – beauty that should result in harmony and respect.

The people around us should see the evidence of changed lives demonstrated by the love of God actively at work in people's lives – in each of our lives.[7]

Sometimes, when following a dream, we take the logical path and it doesn't turn out the way we expect it to. It became clear when reading Richard's sermons and letters that he believed it was God's leading that his church (NDCC) was to be a sort of 'base camp' from which he would venture out to work in Native American ministry. He said, 'New Discovery is in the unique position to be internationally involved in furthering the cause and Kingdom of Christ among Native Indigenous people. Opportunities have been opened to our church to you through me, to be involved in Native ministry in various parts of the world.'[8] Later that year at a church leadership team retreat, Richard presented a 'pivotal document' describing his vision and how he believed it to be connected with his work at NDCC. New Discovery Community Church Leadership Team Retreat Outline:

Nov. 13-14, 1992

To the Leadership Team at NDCC:

This paper represents God's dealing in my life over the past three to five years. It represents who I am in Christ and clearly reflects how I view ministry. It reflects God's gifting, calling, and vision for my life as a leader in the Body of Christ. It also reflects the changes God has made in me.

Kingdom work is an intentional enterprise. It calls for looking ahead, estimating resources, clarifying objectives, and finally moving ahead with purpose.

---

[7] Richard Twiss, 'Where Does Your Neighbor Live?' (sermon presented at New Discovery Community Church, Vancouver, WA, July 15, 1990).

[8] Richard Twiss, 'Get Stirred Up' (sermon presented at New Discovery Community Church, Vancouver, WA, Mar. 15, 1992).

Vision by definition is a reflection of what God wants to accomplish through his people. It is not a concoction of mere men, but God conveying his view of the future to leaders. Visionary people receive their vision from God.

I see the need for New Discovery and the leadership team to embrace and support my personal ministry outside NDCC as a part of the vision of NDCC. My involvement as Executive Director of the North American Native Christian Council (NANCC)[9] will grow in 1993.

I am prepared, I think, for people presently with us, old timers included, who may consider saying 'no' to this vision. That's really OK!

My title in the congregation should be 'presiding elder,' not pastor, because I will be traveling more.

I want to work with a team, a highly committed core. In Alaska they always said a dog sled team was only as fast as its slowest dog. I am looking for a commitment with the knowledge that some sacrifice goes with the turf.[10]

Networking with Others in Native American Ministry

Networking with like-minded people is a good step to take when putting your foot carefully on the next stepping stone toward the fulfillment of your God-given dream.

While still pastoring at New Discovery, Richard began to look for ways to connect with others in Native American Ministry in order to work together and expand effectiveness in reaching people for Christ. He joined and was appointed Executive Director of the North American Native Christian Council (NANCC) and he was active in this group from 1992-1995. His correspondence in that capacity included letters to and from several Native American pastors and leaders of well-known Native ministry organizations. Things went well at first,

---

[9] Richard became executive director of the North American Native Christian Council (NANCC) in 1992. Its headquarters was moved from California to Vancouver, Washington because of Richard's directorship.

[10] Richard Twiss, 'New Discovery Community Church Leadership Team Retreat Outline' (Presentation at New Discovery Community Church Leadership Team Retreat, Nov.13-14, 1992).

and Richard made friends with many who were in agreement with the need for a transition to contextual ministry.

Richard's growing involvement with NANCC and the prominent 'Spiritual Warfare Movement' of the time became evident in his writings. The vision Richard had been given became clearer, and he started outlining his ideas for their implementation.

A Letter to the 'NANCC Guys':

Dec. 6, 1993

The past year has been a memorable one for me. One highlight was traveling to Mongolia. It was my first time out of the U.S. and was a great adventure in the Lord.

Another was traveling to Seoul, Korea, to participate in the International Spiritual Warfare Network Consultation. There are some interesting developments that have come my way that I think could have a bearing on the future and direction of NANCC.

Perhaps six or seven years ago, a conviction began growing in me about marketplace commerce being a modern-day battlefield for Native people. For most tribes, with the disappearance of buffalo and other wild game, the ability of a man to know dignity, integrity, and self-worth by providing for his family and community disappeared. When warfare among tribes stopped, so did a man's ability to gain honor and respect from deeds of bravery and courage. Native men are now without a vehicle to gain pride and honor in our modern world.

I believe God might want us to remember that commerce and trade was also a distinct and valued part of life among Native people of all tribes. I believe that in Christ, commerce can be redeemed as a way for men to once again compete against others for honor and dignity.

I have a friend who is currently involved in a low-cost housing project. His vision is to use business as a church-planting vehicle. At this point, he is pursuing the possibility of setting up his first manufacturing plant on a reservation. He is discussing, with others, the idea of establishing trade relationships among reservations, individual states, and with other countries to provide low-cost housing and build manufacturing plants. This would provide finances for Kingdom work, jobs on the reservation, and would significantly benefit that tribe.

I don't want to 'miss the parade'. If NANCC is not the 'float' for me to join the parade with, then because I want to be in the parade, I'll either find another float or design a new one. I am committed for the long haul to be a team player in this game.

Thanks for putting up with this urban Indian's long rambling letter! God bless you!

Richard Twiss[11]

The following year Richard sent another letter to the NANCC members, this time outlining his vision and goals for them as an organization in 1995:

Dec. 20, 1994

Dear Brothers,

In the desire to continue building long term friendships with other Indigenous leaders in ministry, I thought to send along my ideas about where we should be going as an organization in 1995.

World Christian Indigenous Peoples Conference

Plans have been set in motion already for the Maori to host the first World Christian Indigenous Peoples conference in October of 1996 in Auckland, New Zealand.

We – as NANCC – can play as big a role as we choose in participating at every level of planning, organizing, speaking, etc. This will be a historic gathering of ethnic peoples in furthering God's purposes among Indigenous people. I am one of the international steering committee members.

Reconciliation as a Primary Ministry Focus

The completed work of Jesus Christ on the cross is what has given birth and rise to this reconciliation 'movement'. I will remain

---

[11] Richard Twiss, 'NANCC Guys' letter, 6 December 1993.

strongly committed to and a part of what God is doing in this area of reconciliation – especially as it relates to Native people.

Cultural Authenticity: A Focus on Contextualization

A second passion in my life concerns culture. I feel it is important for me to say I am deeply committed to a more culturally-contextualized expression of the Kingdom of God in and through Native peoples – an expression that will affect a number of issues concerning education, evangelistic methods, theology, and various worship forms and expressions. For me this includes the use of all musical instruments, dance forms, language, music forms, dress, and so on.

I heartily agree with something Adrian Jacobs[12] said to me recently: 'We must be thoroughly biblical and perhaps even conservative in our theology, but as equally strongly liberal in our methodology'. I think we have made a grave error in becoming as conservative in our methods as we are in our theology. Perhaps fear and a lack of trust in the Holy Spirit has kept us at a safe and suspicious distance, in many ways, from our cultures. In some ways this has brought a degree of hypocrisy to how we live out the Kingdom of God in our cultures. I want to be as fully Lakota as I can be, while being fully Christian.

Because the devil is not a creator, he can only pervert and abuse what the Creator has made. The drum, the dance, the gourd, the piano, the cymbal, the guitar, and the saxophone each belong to God. Because the devil has perverted the use of God's drum, people have bought into the lie that the drum is his.

Richard

In the bins we found a hand-written note documenting a vision Richard had concerning the use of the Native American drum in worship. Stapled to it was a long list of Scripture references documenting the use of musical instruments in the Bible.

---

[12] Adrian Jacobs (Ganosono), Turtle Clan, Cayuga Nation, Six Nations Haudenosaunee Confederacy; joint author of the Foreword to Richard Twiss, *Rescuing the Gospel from the Cowboys*, and author of the poem, 'You Just Ghosted', among others.

Drum Vision

In the vision I had I saw a Native drum – it was held upright – before the Lord. My prayer began to be that the Holy Spirit would be *loosed* through the music of the drum. The drum was being offered to the Lord.

I felt that there was a curse on the drum so that it is silent before the Lord. It is not being offered to the Lord. It cannot be used for the purpose it was created for. All instruments are created by God for worship – to carry the anointing, to *loose* the Holy Spirit (like when David played for Saul) – to glorify God. But the drum is silent in worship and the Spirit that is longing, even weeping, to blow over the people is still.

I believe that this curse has been placed on the Native drum *by the people of God* – somehow – in fear or ignorance or hate – nonetheless a curse. The curse needs to be broken and the drum offered to the Lord as an instrument of worship.

I saw a picture of the curse being broken – all kinds of people worshipping and dancing to the drums – not just Native Americans. And the Holy Spirit just fell – crash! Everyone was affected. It was so awesome and powerful.

Let your glory fall![13]

Richard also wrote the following:

I have a personal conviction that until Christian Natives bring their unique expression of Christ and his Kingdom into the mainstream of the evangelical Christian community, or the Body of Christ, the Body is handicapped. It is deprived of an essential ingredient without which the Bride can never become fully prepared or readied for the coming groom. The Bride is to be whole, without spot or wrinkle, and with nothing missing. We should not continue to be an 'Anglo' expression culturally, when God did not make us that way.

The burden of responsibility for this perhaps misrepresentative expression of 'Christ in us' is now passing from the paternalism of the early ones [Native American believers] to us. The cause of

---

[13] Vision recorded among Dr Twiss's notes, 1990s.

this deprivation is shifting from them to us. We, the Christian Native leaders in the church in North America today, will be the ones doing the 'holding back from' what the Body of Christ so desperately needs to be made ready. In Psalm 137 there is a lament of a people taken captive who had put away their old songs from back home while in their captivity. The church needs some of our 'new old songs'.

I know there are many legitimate concerns and questions we all have about some of these things, but brothers, God will help us! Because He made us the way we are, he will complete what he began in us long before the first missionaries landed here. From before the foundations of the world, he has prepared good works for us as a people group to accomplish.

I have honestly and openly shared some of the things in my heart with you through this letter. I'd much rather do it over a cup of coffee sometime, though. If you feel led to dialogue with me about any of these things, I would be blessed.

Love in Christ,

Richard[14]

There were members of NANCC who were strongly opposed to Native American contextual ministry. Accusations toward Richard regarding syncretism began and then escalated. The inclusion of Native cultural styles of worship – especially dance and the use of the Native drum – were condemned by some of them. Because of this, Richard resigned as director.

So, continuing to pursue his dream needed to take another direction – another 'float' in the parade.

---

[14] Richard Twiss, Proposal for NANCC 1995 Goals, 20 December 1994.

A Prophetic Church: Reconciliation
The message of reconciliation is a call from the Father's heart to
a broken world. The call from a broken world is for Christians,
the church, to be involved, modeling reconciliation in difficult situations with difficult people.

*The potential power inherent in a unified body of Christ is dissipated
through ideological splits, theological spats, and philosophical severs. The
smallest nonessential differences are reason for digging in our heels, turning
dialogue into debate, declaring winners, and by extension, losers.*

We can be confident that Jesus can help and comfort us because he knows what we are going through because he suffered as
a human just like we do. Jesus had to become one of us first, before he could show us the way out of our dilemma.
Jesus is my kind of guy! [15]

Connections with Others in Native American Ministry
No doubt the circumstances surrounding the resignation from
NANCC were disappointing, but, if at first you don't find your per-
manent 'niche', move on. Richard moved on by accepting employ-
ment with the International Bible Society (IBS) in March of 1995.
This was the next step in fulfilling his dream from God.

Richard continued reaching out to others interested in or working
in contextual ministry as he began his full-time work with IBS. The
following letter underlines his growing passion for contextualization
and his desire to form a community of contextual ministry leaders.
It was written during his employment with IBS.

*A North American Coalition for the 'Acculturation of Christianity & Na-
tive Cultures for the 21st Century'*

Letter to a Group of Native Contextual Ministers:

May 5, 1995

Greetings brother and sisters,

---

[15] Richard Twiss, 'A Prophetic Church: Reconciliation' (sermon presented at
New Discovery Community Church, Vancouver, WA, July 10, 1994).

It seems to me the Holy Spirit is putting together a coalition of Christian leaders who want to challenge some of our existing paradigms for ministry among Native peoples. It also seems that the Holy Spirit is giving us new eyes through which to view the importance of our cultures in God's purposes.

This letter is a first attempt to establish an ongoing dialogue among those of us, for whom it would seem, God has given a growing passion to see a more authentic Native expression of Christianity among the Indigenous peoples of North America. As I have talked with each of you, it has become clear to me that the Holy Spirit is connecting many of us together from a wide variety of different streams of ministry, traditions, denominations, geographic regions, and so on, to pursue a common vision. A vision and dream of seeing our Native people come to Christ in greater numbers, discipled to be fully devoted followers of Jesus Christ and equipped to lead others in serving the Creator's eternal purposes all the days of their lives – a dream of seeing our cultures redeemed and incarnated through Christ to more fully reflect his glory and purposes for his people in the earth.

All of us are saying that bigger, better, and more of the 'same' is not going to necessarily produce results any different than we've had the past 400 years and certainly in our lifetimes.

The bad things grow worse and the church struggles with only minimal fruit at best in Indian Country. If God does not help us, we will continue down this long painful road. Native cultures have not been created as sons of perdition! There is a better way in Christ. Our cultures have been infused with values, customs, and worship forms by God himself to glorify Jesus Christ.

There are great and powerful winds of change blowing in our direction. Institutions, ministry philosophies, theologies, and people/leaders are all in the process of being positioned and repositioned, rearranged, disassembled, retooled, and molded by God the Father to accommodate his plans and purposes.

A Native American Theology is Being Born!!

A few of us met recently in Colorado Springs to initiate a process to convene a North American Symposium. The pursuit of this vision cannot be perceived as one person's, or one organization's, or one denomination's project. It has to be seen as a Native inspired, initiated, led, and sustained, movement! Not Native only, but led – in intimate partnership with our non-Indian believers!

The big question: With the current prevailing views of Native culture and ministry philosophies, 'What would the "First Nations" in North America look like culturally if every Native person were a Christian?' Would Native people simply assimilate into the mainstream evangelical community? Let's think through what we believe!

Prayer and intercession are equally as important as the academic disciplines in this pursuit. We are confronting centuries-old strongholds that are not going to simply disappear.

Your friend and servant,

Richard Twiss[16]

Richard believed the next step toward the fruition of his vision would be through his work with IBS. But when it came to contextualization, they preferred to remain 'neutral'.[17] Richard was anything but 'neutral' about contextualization!
From contacts made through his work at IBS, Richard's network reached to First Nations workers in contextual ministry in Canada. They too were being inundated with accusations of syncretism.

Oct. 16, 1995

Greetings Brothers [IBS],

We need to formally, amongst ourselves, decide what our posture and involvement is going to be concerning contextualization. For my part, I see that IBS is in a wonderful God-given unique position to play a very significant role in serving God's purposes among Native people. How? – by providing a relatively neutral platform for this type of activity to take place. We can assist this new movement in both a catalytic and facilitative capacity, in partnership with other organizations, gatherings, and publications. This will, in effect, lessen some of the existing Native ministry

---

[16] Richard Twiss, letter to a group of contextual ministers, 5 May 1995.
[17] IBS, letter to Richard Twiss, May 1995.

organizations' influence, and as I've heard, intimidation, in order for this growing grassroots contextualization movement to gain momentum through God's blessing and leading. The hoped-for end result will be that the remaining 97% of Native people will be impacted for Jesus Christ!

Blessings to you brothers,

Richard Twiss[18]

Resistance to Contextualization and Getting IBS's Native American Ministry Department Organized

Resistance to contextualization continued, but Richard pressed toward the goal of the dream given to him by God.

Letter to IBS:

Oct. 20, 1995

Greetings,

On Monday I talked with a Native colleague at length. He told me of a group of eight Native leaders who met together to share their dreams and desires about contextualization in Native American ministry. I was invited to join them, but couldn't attend. My friend said his group is concerned about how to break past the current leadership mindset toward Indian ministry.

He said he doesn't agree with 'where they are at' and sees their thinking as a several-generation old 'Anglo-missionary' mindset that has become a hindrance to effective cross-cultural ministry.

My friend thinks publishing a quarterly journal is a good direction to head in with this contextualization movement. He made the following observations: There is politicking involved in Indian ministry today, there is a perceived threat of losing control or influence among some of the current Native leaders, and he encouraged me not to be disheartened.

Another friend called me this morning, regarding getting organized for the World Christian Gathering of Indigenous People

---

[18] Richard Twiss, letter to IBS 16 October 1995.

(WCGIP) in New Zealand. He said they have already had a tremendous international response, and inquiries are coming in from countries in Africa, Sweden, Japan, the Philippines, Asia, and throughout the South Pacific. He said that Desmond Tutu will be speaking to close the conference.

What they are after is a historical 'gathering of the tribes' type of environment and experience – not a typical Christian conference. They are thinking a regional delegation would have a day or evening to do their thing – preach, sing, dance, worship, teach, perform in full costume, or whatever they felt led by the Lord to do. He said people will be encouraged to bring crafts to sell, trade, and teach others to make. In the evenings would be much eating, storytelling, and laughter – a truly Indigenous people's gathering – sounds like a major blast to me.

Love,

Richard[19]

It was clear that Richard was beginning to have a wide view of the 'big picture' of Native American contextual ministry. Acts 1.8 says, 'But you will receive power when the Holy Spirit comes on you; and you will be my witnesses in Jerusalem, and in all Judea and Samaria, and to the ends of the earth'. Richard took this to heart and expanded his contextual horizons. IBS was *international* after all!

Richard was starting to 'flesh out' his vision of how to reach the Indigenous world – first starting here 'at home' in the U.S., and then around the world by designing specific programs to be implemented through IBS. Project Rational Form for IBS by Richard Twiss 1996-1997:

Vision Trips – Short-term Trips to Native American Reservations

The vision trips (for IBS supporters) will enable people to experience or witness a sense of stepping back into time in U.S. history, the state of the Native American Christian church, being in a 'foreign culture' and listening to another language right in America, gaining an insider's view of the needs and possibilities of ministry,

---

[19] Richard Twiss, letter to IBS, 20 October 1995.

and to some degree developing a feeling of the brokenness of the people.

The vision trips will be promoted in part as an educational cross-cultural training school experience. They will be provided with suggested pre-trip reading materials and on-site interactive study materials covering cultural worldview distinctives and values, U.S. missionary history, the history of the Indigenous peoples of the Americas, and building relationships across ethnic differences.

We will look at some Native American spirituality that is thoroughly evangelical and biblical in principle. Native people don't divide life into sacred and secular spheres, but view their religious experience as something that is a daily reality, and they place a great emphasis and value on enjoying friends and relatives – relationships versus accomplishments and status. This will hopefully result in a time of prayer, communion, and reconciliation with what God is doing and saying among Native peoples.

We will be involved in some type of community or church service project.

Banquets: Fundraisers for IBS

We will have Native American performers as part of the evening program, as well as Native music, dance, storytelling, and an example of a redeemed social ceremony.

Native Worship Music Project

Worship music is a powerful medium. We believe now is a perfect time to introduce what we believe will be the first Native American worship CD in America. Our worship tape will be written, performed, and produced with the vision to see Native cultural music styles and lyrics used to bless and edify the church in America. Some of the song lyrics will be scripture passages translated into tribal languages.

Travel Ministry Team

Our traveling team will demonstrate how one can be used as a significant instrument for God's praise and purposes. This will essentially be a performing arts ministry. Its primary purpose will be to communicate the Good News of Jesus Christ and the dynamics of the Kingdom relative to First Nations peoples.

The team will be used for fundraising, evangelistic outreaches on reservations or urban areas targeting Native audiences, and to target New Agers and 'seekers' through Native cultural performances.

The team will also be used internationally to demonstrate how God has redeemed and prepared a place for Native cultures to be used to reach the peoples of the world for Jesus Christ. This will help raise the self-esteem and sense of value in the Lord among Native people 'back home,' and cause the Church in America to reconsider the place of Native peoples in the Church. We will draw on the strong attraction, respect, and curiosity that Native American culture enjoys around the world.[20]

Publishing as a Means of Spreading Native American Contextual Ministry

While at IBS, Richard worked on the inception and 'launch' of their *Native Wind Magazine*. Richard knew the 'power of the pen' in getting out the message of contextualization. There was concern among some that the contents of *Native Wind* would support only the contextual end of the Native ministry spectrum. IBS reiterated their desire to remain neutral in order to work with the entire Native ministry community.[21]

At about the same time, Richard received a reply from the Associate Editor of *Charisma Magazine*, asking him to write an article, with the possibility of a monthly article in the future. He was asked to write from the 'passions of his heart' on Native issues. Richard saw this as an excellent opportunity to communicate the IBS vision and promote *Native Wind* on a national level. Richard did end up writing a monthly column for *Charisma* called 'Smoke Signals' from 2001-2002.[22]

---

[20] Richard Twiss, 'Project Rationale for 1996-1997', to IBS, likely December 1996.

[21] IBS, letter to Richard Twiss, 22 April 1996.

[22] Richard Twiss, letter to IBS, 15 July 1996.

Association with Promise Keepers

During Richard's work as Native American Director for IBS, he and nineteen other Native American leaders were invited by Promise Keepers (PK) to 'discuss developing a Northwest Network of Native ministry leaders within PK'.[23]

> During the 1990s there was a growing recognition of 'neglect' on the part of national evangelical Christian ministries concerning the contribution of Native American leaders and voices. Promise Keepers (PK) was another organization having 'racial reconciliation' as one of their 'guiding values'.

> In 2000 I was formally invited to speak at the Albuquerque event. Shortly before the event, however, I received a call from a PK senior staff member informing me that some Native ministry leaders were threatening to boycott the event if I were allowed to be a platform speaker. In the 'spirit of unity' they asked me to voluntarily withdraw. There was no mention of dialogue or a meeting to resolve any differences in the 'spirit of reconciliation'. They paid me my agreed-to honorarium and I 'voluntarily' withdrew.[24]

Richard and Katherine continued their journey toward their destined call by moving to Plummer, Idaho, to the Coeur d'Alene Indian Reservation, to work with IBS. His sphere of influence expanded during his time there, but it became increasingly clear that they were to return to Vancouver, Washington, and launch their own ministry, 'Wiconi International' – in order to be free to follow God's leading in their lives. It seemed like Richard and Katherine would soon see the fulfillment of their God-given dream.

Discussion Questions

1. Discuss how Dr Twiss overcame opposition on his journey from Western-trained evangelical to Native American contextual minister.

2. Do you see these types of barriers as still prevalent in the church? What do you see as the most challenging obstacle to contextual ministry today?

---

[23] Richard Twiss, letter to representatives of Promise Keepers, 28 August 1996.
[24] Richard Twiss, *Rescuing the Gospel from the Cowboys*, pp. 176-77.

4

THE FOUNDING OF WICONI INTERNATIONAL

*There is a relationship to divine call that we must embrace and remain
committed to all of our lives as followers of Jesus!* [1]

It looked as if Richard and Katherine had come to the 'end of the
road' for their dream when they chose to move on after his employment with the International Bible Society (IBS). But he continued to
stay focused on the 'goal set before him' – the dream placed before
him by God. Each organization Richard worked for was a 'stepping
stone' on the way to the fruition of the dream – the end goal. He
learned more as he progressed on his journey. Each organization had
provided education, networking, and opportunities to expand the
message of Native American contextual ministry.

He kept aiming to 'hit his stride' in a ministry format that matched
what Holy Spirit had revealed to him. Already-established ministries
were true to their own missions, but really weren't the 'best fit' for
Richard and Katherine.

Through Richard's letters we could see the common thread and
ideas forming over the years. Each step on their journey was important in the learning process and the fine tuning of the ultimate
goal of their dream.

It became increasingly clear that founding their own ministry
would allow them the flexibility to 'enlarge their territory' using the
knowledge they had gained. They could also network with like-
minded colleagues and take advantage of opportunities for the use

---

[1] Richard Twiss, 'The Cream Always Rises' (sermon presented to New Discovery Community Church, Vancouver, WA, June 30, 1992).

of media and public speaking. Sometimes you just have to get out of the boat!

During his time working as the Executive Director for the North American Native Christian Council (NANCC), Richard composed his projected goals for 1996. This document outlined his ideas for the transformation of Native American ministry into a more effective force for the salvation of Indigenous people.

It is interesting now, in hindsight, to see that Richard and Katherine accomplished, or started to implement, all the goals listed in the NANCC document before Richard's passing. Each ministry focus mentioned in the planning report is now available for use (or is being used) by the current and next generations of ministry practitioners. God is faithful to perform what he has promised.

On the Road to the Fulfillment of the Promised Dream: Ideas Implemented after the Founding of Wiconi

'But you will receive power when the Holy Spirit comes on you; and you will be my witnesses in Jerusalem, and in all Judea and Samaria, and to the ends of the earth' (Acts 1.8, NIV). Richard outlined his ministry goals for NANCC, ranging from ideas to impact the nation, the continent, and then internationally in a plan similar to that put forth in the book of Acts:

> As I see it, central to the big picture is *Native people emerging as a recognized, valued, needed, and vitally-functioning part of the Body of Christ.* We must recognize that Native ministry work requires equal emphasis on both the rural/reservation and the urban populations.

> The following points are those that I personally feel most strongly about being involved in: Developing a functional network of Native leaders for the purpose of strategizing about more fruitful methods of evangelism in Native work, building a national intercessory prayer base, helping to connect Native leaders to the evangelical mainstream, and serving Native leaders in fulfilling their callings and ministries to the Body of Christ.[2]

---

[2] Richard Twiss, 'Native American Ministry Goals', paper submitted to NANCC, June 1995.

In 1996, fifty-two North American Native leaders attended the inaugural World Christian Gathering of Indigenous People (WCGIP), hosted by the Maori people in New Zealand. More than 2,000 people from thirty-two countries attended. For eight days, tribal people worshipped Jesus using their Indigenous music, dance, clothing, ceremony, ritual, languages and stories as cultural expressions of their biblical faith. In 1998 leaders from North America hosted the Gathering in Rapid City, South Dakota. This served as a major catalytic assembly for Native leaders exploring these new possibilities, with many meeting for the first time.

On the heels of the WCGIP in Rapid City, Wiconi International convened twenty 'Many Nations, One Voice' celebrations in eighteen cities across North America from 1999 to 2005, which served as significant catalytic events to introduce and promote these new ideas. Thousands of people attended these venues across the United States and Canada, many of whom then went home and began their own contextualization efforts in their local contexts.[3]

Wiconi International then took on the primary responsibility of planning and organizing the Many Nations 1 Voice (MN1V) celebrations.[4]

International Networking and Education
Friendships developed during the WCGIP events and MN1V Celebrations influenced the formation of the North American Institute for Indigenous Theological Studies (NAIITS):

Also of great importance to me is to assist in forming an international coalition of Indigenous leaders world-wide, to be vitally involved in developing a coalition for the formation of a North American Native theology, examining from a theological, missiological, anthropological and historical perspective, the place of redeeming Native culture for the purposes of reaching lost Native people and equipping the Church to become all God intends for her to be.[5]

---

[3] Richard Twiss, 'Making Jesus Known in Knowable Ways', *Mission Frontiers* (September-October 2010), p. 8. http://www.missionfrontiers.org/issue/article/making-jesus-known-in-knowable-ways.

[4] Twiss, *Rescuing the Gospel from the Cowboys*, pp. 139, 140.

[5] Twiss, 'Native American Ministry Goals'.

In 1999, the controversial issue of contextualization of theology by and for Native North Americans prompted a small group of Native evangelicals to explore ways to address the issue. The church had struggled to make sense of the issue – a problem to which many had been both witting and unwitting contributors. Finding little in print that addressed the theological and biblical issues at hand, this small band determined to gather a group of people together to explore and write on the issue of contextualization – of culture and faith.

NAIITS was born in response to the inability of the Christian evangelical church to include Indigenous peoples in a manner that affirmed who their Creator has shaped them to be. NAIITS personnel believe Indigenous followers of Jesus have something to contribute to the wider community of faith in terms of theology, most particularly to the Indigenous community.[6]

The Need for Higher Education and a Body of Literature

Richard knew formal education would be a crucial factor in being able to contribute to a needed body of literature to educate future leaders in contextual ministry:

> *To this end, formal education and training becomes a high priority for me.* [Richard would eventually earn his DMiss through Asbury Theological Seminary, Wilmore, Kentucky.] My additional goals are to help to produce written material for the Christian Native community in developing new models, strategies, and philosophies for ministry, help produce various educational materials to inform the non-Native Christian community about the needs and current situation among Native peoples, assist in the publication of an *Indian Life* type magazine,[7] write and have other Native writers produce articles for various Christian periodicals, help produce Scripture products for evangelism using Native culture as a vehicle for communicating Christ and his Word to both the Anglo and Native communities, produce literary and possibly artistic products by Natives for non-Native secular audiences who have a curiosity and attraction to Indian religion and culture, and work toward the

---

[6] 'A Brief History of NAIITS', *NAIITS: An Indigenous Learning Community*, accessed Mar. 20, 2017, naiits.com/history/.

[7] Indian Life Ministries publishes *Indian Life Newspaper* and other printed ministry resources, indianlife.org.

long-term vision of seeing a Native College/Cultural Center established.[8]

The Publishing Journey Begins for Richard

Richard devoted much time to writing and encouraging his colleagues to do the same – to provide the needed 'products' for effective ministry to Native people. In 1998 he authored *Culture, Christ, & Kingdom Study Guide* for use in workshops. The same year he also published *Dancing Our Prayers* in response to accusations of syncretism. *One Church Many Tribes: Following Jesus the Way God Made You* was published in 2000.

Richard wrote a bi-monthly column called 'Smoke Signals' for *Charisma Magazine* from 2001-2002. He wrote articles for many other magazines, anthologies, and scholarly journals (such as the NAIITS journals).

National and International Outreach through the Performing Arts

'Dancing Our Prayers' performing arts teams were formed through Wiconi as a witness to both Native and non-Native audiences. Richard lectured in or led these Native cultural teams to Pakistan, China, Israel, France, Peru, Australia, Tibet, South Africa, and more than a dozen other nations, addressing issues of spirituality, justice, and extending the hope for a better world to tens of thousands.

The Ministry of Reconciliation

In the same NANCC document, Richard expressed his desire 'to remain active and involved in the ministry of reconciliation'. He later became a member of the Board of Directors of the Christian Community Development Association (CCDA),[9] and also taught diversity workshops for a variety of organizations. He was well-received – as enthusiastic reviews indicated:

> I think I was impacted most by the boarding school history and Richard's discussion about why it does not make sense to just forget about the past and 'get on with it'. I was enlightened by his theory of the impact the boarding schools had on a generation of people – the fact that these individuals were robbed of the chance to learn how to be parents and raise a family and how this affects

---

[8] Twiss, 'Native American Ministry Goals'.
[9] www.ccda.org.

the entire Native American people today. I know there is no magical answer about how to align everybody's 'world view,' but I wish there was. I would just like to thank Richard for taking the time to come and speak with us and for being so open. It was one of the best diversity workshops I have attended.

'John'[10]

In 2004, Richard and Katherine recognized a desire for closer community among the now-connected Native ministry leaders and their families, and Wiconi Family Camp resulted from that vision. The following year the '*Mni Wiconi Wacipi Living Waters Powwow*' was added to the family camp event. 'Initially we thought in terms of it being a Christian powwow. It is now considered a community-centered, intertribal traditional powwow where Jesus is honored, but not a 'Christian' powwow. By that I mean it is not organized specifically as a Christian gathering or event'.[11] Wiconi Family Camp/ powwow provides a place to experience contextual family life in a community environment.

Challenges Concurrent with the Blessings
All these blessings showed that fulfillment of their dream was underway. But seasons tend to cycle and overlap. The challenges of the topic of syncretism were revisited in the early 2000s and continued until Richard's passing. During that time frame, there were occasions when someone would call ahead when Richard was scheduled as a guest speaker. They would 'strongly caution' the well-known Christian academic institutions about allowing him to speak. Usually the institutions dismissed such behavior, but sometimes Richard was removed from their list of speakers.

Richard recognized that making the choice to follow his dream from God would thrust him into the 'public eye' – and that there would likely be consequences. He said, 'A commitment to God will plunder your ambition and play havoc with your privacy – a commitment to God will destroy the privacy of your life to a great degree.

---

[10] Review from a participant at a diversity lunch presented by Richard Twiss in Vancouver, Washington, November 1997.
[11] Twiss, *Rescuing the Gospel from the Cowboys*, p. 144.

When you commit yourself to God, you are no longer a private person, you are part of a purpose'.[12] Letter from Richard Twiss to Ministry Colleagues in a 'Major Christian Organization':[13]

Jan. 14, 2003

Dear Friends,

You are all aware (to varying degrees) of some of the tensions in Native ministry with various leaders over issues of faith and culture. These tensions extend far beyond the borders of the U.S. and Canada and impact Indigenous/tribal peoples globally. Perhaps I should be flattered, as my name seems to come up quite frequently in many of those conversations.

I believe, however, they are far more than localized cultural issues personified in a certain individual's ideas or philosophically different approach to ministry, but have underneath them some far-reaching spiritual implications.

The opposition we face is far more than a debate about feathers, symbols, and instruments because it is not a flesh and blood debate. Behind this conversation is a strong religious spirit entwined with issues of *territory, authority, and face*. It is a subversive thing that only sows *suspicion, division, and antagonism* among believers. Though frequently maligned and organizationally marginalized, I refuse to allow that to become part of how I go about my Father's business.

I want you to know these tensions have dramatically escalated to the point where those who disagree with my/our perspectives on some of these issues are now sending communiques to major Christian organizations charging me/us of being false teachers, teaching heresy, and promoting sin in the church.

I look forward to hearing back from you.

Many blessings as we journey together in Christ,

Richard Twiss[14]

---

[12] Richard Twiss, 'Concern for One Another' (sermon presented at New Discovery Community Church, Vancouver, WA, Oct. 8, 1989).

[13] Name of 'Organization' withheld by authors.

[14] Richard Twiss, letter to ministry colleagues, 14 January 2003.

One can 'hear' the frustration between the lines in this letter – probably the opposition *was* infuriating at times. But to Richard's credit, he later said in 2012:

> This has to be okay for me at some level, if I am going to love my neighbor and not be perpetually disappointed or judgmental of their experience. There are untold numbers of Native people in those churches who would testify to how Jesus genuinely saved them from enslavement to alcohol, violence, or drug abuse, and set them free to be better human beings. That being said, it is a kind of Christianity that is waning, but will nonetheless still out-live me. The hope for *this* project [contextualization] is that it will encourage and empower the next generations of Native followers of Jesus who are growing disillusioned with that old wineskin.[15]

The Need for Native American Contextual Ministry

God is good to give us balance in our lives. Fulfillment of your dream will eventually balance out the obstacles you had to overcome on the way. In spite of the negative comments, accusations, misunderstandings, and outright spiritual attacks, contextual ministry is desperately needed to reach that remaining '97%' Richard talked about.

Included in the bins full of sermons and letters were many folders containing endorsements from people famous in the world of ministry and missions. More importantly, there were many letters expressing profound thanks for Richard's inspired words in *One Church, Many Tribes*, in addition to his many other writings and speaking engagements. Many of the letters contain testimonies of changed lives:

November 2000

Dear Mr Twiss,

I recently came across your book *One Church Many Tribes*. What a blessing it has been to me! I have been struggling for many years trying to reconcile my faith with my culture. I am a Native woman living on a reservation. As far as I know, I am the only Christian in my family.

My family is very resistant for the reasons you recite in your book – they see Christianity as 'White man's' religion. They are living in

---

[15] Twiss, *Rescuing the Gospel from the Cowboys*, p. 216.

darkness and the children are following the same path as the previous generations, falling into drugs and alcohol – they need *Jesus!* – and to know the love of the Father.

Thank you so much for your book. I haven't finished it yet; I can hardly put it down!

'Jane'[16]

The above composite letter mirrors many of those expressing gratitude for Richard's teachings and for the words and views eloquently expressed in *One Church, Many Tribes.*

We have seen the 'fruit' of these ministries and the message of contextual ministry used to share the gospel effectively. It is clear that there continues to be a need to 'become all things to all people so that by all possible means I might save some' (1 Cor. 9.22).

All of the God-given blessings resulting from the work of Wiconi, NAIITS, and all the other endeavors Richard was involved in, produced and continue to provide fruitful ministry results.

Our own lives have been changed by the grace and education generously extended to us by Richard, Katherine, and our other friends in contextual ministry – an indication of a season of dream fulfillment in *our* lives too. But after a season of fruitfulness, we were all 'slammed' by the shock of Richard's unexpected passing.

Discussion Questions

1. Dr Twiss progressed from one 'stepping stone' to another on his journey to the fulfillment of his calling. Discuss your own journey and the stepping stones to your calling so far.

2. Many of Dr Twiss's goals were fulfilled during his lifetime. Some are in progress now or have yet to be completed. What can you learn about God's timing for your own calling through Dr Twiss's journey?

---

[16] Letter to Richard Twiss from a Native woman, 2000.

5

Now What? Our Entry into Publishing

The Self-published Version of *Rescuing Theology from the Cowboys*

It seemed as if we had hit a brick wall. It looked like our dream from God could be over. While still reeling from the tragedy of Richard's passing, we were asked by Wiconi if we could have an updated self-published version of *Cowboys* ready in time for Richard's memorial service the next month. Many people had asked to have copies available there.

The manuscript was 'raw' and Richard had added much text until the last few days. We worked late at night doing as much as we could to get it ready in time.

The local Vancouver print shop was a God-send and had printed Richard's earlier self-published version. During this process, all 'hell' suddenly broke loose, as blatant spiritual warfare was launched against all involved in the editing or printing process. We had to break the manuscript into separate documents because our older computer couldn't handle a manuscript this large – scary messages about 'corrupted files' sent chills down my spine! We merged as much as the computer could handle. It was a bit like doing a jigsaw puzzle, making sure all the pieces were in the right place! The day the book was to be printed, the print shop experienced a power outage – nearly preventing publication in time for the memorial service. The Wiconi staff put out an emergency prayer request and their prayers prevailed. The power came back on and the printer offered to stay overtime to finish the job.

More than one thousand people attended the memorial service in Vancouver, and hundreds more watched by live-streaming. The atmosphere was surreal to me – I just couldn't grasp the fact that Richard was gone. It seemed like we would wake up the next morning and he would be there as if nothing had happened.

Merely two days before Richard was stricken he had sent us a 'big project,' as he put it, including instructions as to how he wanted the book to be completed – what a gift from God! The book was to be a sort of hybrid: part textbook and part narrative stories. *Overall,* it is the history of the Native American Contextual Movement. We continued to copyedit and fact check – adding citations from authors only mentioned by name, sometimes only by first name.

Richard's personal assistant and one of the Twiss sons helped by 'unlocking' Richard's laptop so we could work from his most recent version of the manuscript. Katherine gave us the bins full of Richard's unpublished sermons and other documents – trusting us with his words. We used some of those documents and also Internet searches looking for the sources of incomplete citations.

We did our best in the few weeks we had to get the updated self-published version ready. There was still quite a bit of work to be done before the book would be ready for professional publication. We believed that would happen eventually.

After the memorial service, Ray and I worked on our days off for about a year prepping the manuscript for eventual professional publication. That's how long the various assignments and the 'big project' required. Richard had been published before, including *One Church Many Tribes: Following Jesus the Way God Made You.* He knew how much work and time were involved getting a book ready for publication – we were babes in the woods. We had absolutely no idea. Looking back on it now, it was a blessing in disguise. Typing and editing Richard's 'last words' was our way of navigating the grieving process.

Diving into Our Calling and a Glimpse into the Publishing World

Are You Serious? The Life-changing Phone Call

In May of 2014, Katherine called to tell us InterVarsity Press had accepted a proposal for the publication of the *Cowboys* book. She said she believed we 'knew the book better than anyone else on the planet' since we had been working on it with Richard. She wanted to know if we would work with InterVarsity in the publishing process on her behalf.

We believed this to be God's leading and chose to follow this continuing journey of our dream from God and to the fulfillment of our promise to Richard. Perhaps our call to serve Native American people was to be mainly through the written word and the publishing process.

Little Did We Know How Little We Knew

Overwhelmed and Panic Stricken!

Thus began the initial correspondence with our first project editor and then our permanent project editor at IVP – our much appreciated Al Hsu. He asked Katherine and us who was to be IVP's contact person or people – those responsible for changes, updates, corrections, needed rewrites, adding citations, and so on. Katherine asked that we work with IVP to complete these requirements. She remained a part of the email circle of communications throughout the process. We gladly agreed because we knew Richard's words would impact generations of Indigenous people for Christ, and because we wanted to honor our brother. This was the next step for us in following our dream from God.

How Far Can a Person Be S-T-R-E-T-C-H-E-D?

What is an Author Input Form?

InterVarsity asked us questions such as, 'Who is this book for?' We wondered: 'How do we put ourselves into shoes (moccasins!) this big – Richard's shoes?' 'How do we get "into his head"?' All these thoughts and questions swirled in our *own* heads after receiving the 'Author Input Form' from InterVarsity. Pray. Again. And as many times as it takes. Ask Holy Spirit what he wants and what Richard would have wanted, and then run it by Katherine.

Focus on the Next Generation

Who *is* the *Cowboys* book for? We knew Richard wanted the book to appeal to a general audience, but also to be used as a textbook. He was passionate about reaching people for Christ and 'passing the baton' to the next generation for the continuation of contextual ministry.

Native thought sees us as connected with those who have gone before us, those who are with us, and those who are yet to come.[1] Richard worked hard to benefit the next generation.

He was a pastor, a professor at Portland State University and NAIITS, and a board member for many academic institutions and community organizations such as the Christian Community Development Association (Chicago) and Bakke Graduate University (Seattle). He worked on behalf of young people as a board member for the Native American Youth and Family Center (NAYA) in Portland, Oregon. Through Wiconi he was also spearheading a future project called 'Salmon Nation'. It was to be:

> A dynamic, multicultural internship program for emerging leaders between the ages of 18-30 who commit to live and learn to become better humans as they engage in and develop their passion for community development. They will increase their capacity, love deeply, serve generously, care sacrificially, walk respectfully, and embrace the other as they serve Native Americans in the Portland, Oregon metro area.[2]

We pray that someone will eventually 'pick up the baton' for this program and impact future generations – as Richard envisioned.

So, how could we effectively send Richard's message to students? They would learn through the included history and the 'hearts' of the people interviewed in the Sweat Lodge Ceremony described in Chapter 3 of *Cowboys*. They would also have the opportunity to look up the contextual practitioners mentioned in the book and read the books listed in the bibliography.

Normally an *author* writes about his or her passion for the book during this section of the publishing process, but we didn't have an author to do that. Having learned from Richard and our friends in

[1] Richard Twiss, 'Three Past and Three Future: Leadership from Dr. Richard Leo Twiss' (presentation at the Beyond Colorblind 2013 conference at Gordon College, 2013). https://youtu.be/IkjSA6x UHms, Accessed Apr. 30, 2017.
[2] Richard Twiss, 'Salmon Nation Handbook', www.wiconi.com, 2011, Introduction.

contextual ministry, and seen the fruitful results of that, we can honestly say this is ministry *we too* are passionate about.

What a learning process and an unexpected journey we were privileged to enter into! It was a whole new world for us. We gained great respect for the level of excellence required by InterVarsity Press. It also meant much to us knowing that we were working with Christian believers.

The Big Moment Arrives!

OK, so then we waited for IVP's copyeditor to return the manuscript we had worked on for six months with Richard, and then another year polishing for future professional publication. We naively thought there wouldn't be much left to do – after all, we had spent a great deal of time trying to honor our dear friend and had completed the work to the best of our ability!

Then came the wakeup call. Technical writing and newspaper editing are *not* the same as copyediting for a professional publishing company! We had *no* idea how much is involved in the book-publishing process – and I suspect what we experienced was the tip of the iceberg.

There were essentially multitudes of 'red marks' throughout the returned manuscript. We even had a deadline for each assignment in the process and they expected us to meet them! I felt like I remember feeling when getting a paper marked in red ink back from a middle school English teacher! I took a very deep breath and prayed for HELP – you know – one of those prayers silently shouted in desperation!

God was and *is* faithful. He graciously answered me by reminding me of the process I use when working on botanical paintings – 'do what you know first'. I read and re-read the questions, comments, and requests. I 'fixed' what I knew first, then worked on successive sections of more complicated queries and made changes to fit IVP style requirements. There were *more* citations to complete. After every section of work was completed, Ray copyedited. We went from one stepping stone to the next.

The Internet is my Friend

Since *Cowboys* is mainly a history of the Native American Contextualization Movement, Richard of course cited many historic documents and history books. Much text had been added in the days before his passing. We knew this because we had worked on the manuscript with him as a shared document. We noticed when he was writing and making changes because it showed up on our computer's desktop. It was as if he were a 'man on a mission from Creator' in his last few weeks here on earth. Saying his work on the book was 'fast and furious' would be the understatement of all understatements.

Well, all those added words needed citations. We knew from experience with him that Richard was faithful to give people credit for their words and work. He just wasn't here long enough to finish the job.

So, the internet searches resumed. I would cut and paste fragments of sentences and probably eighty percent of the time would find what I was looking for. Some of the authors quoted were personal friends of Richard's, and the Wiconi staff gave us access to contact information for them. They were gracious and replied with much patience; their help was invaluable.

Ray works in our library system – talk about a source of information! He has access to almost anything in print locally, or through interlibrary loans. Ray found copies of many of the books Richard used for research that way. Some of the books we already owned.

What are 'Permissions' and do we Really Need Them?

Of course, we agree that people should get credit for their work. We knew that books are covered by copyright law. What we didn't know is that there are limits on how many words can be directly quoted without seeking permission and sometimes payments must be made to their publishers.

Let the Word Counts Begin!

Our friends at InterVarsity gave us guidelines for obtaining permission from the appropriate publishers. Permission is required for quotes greater than 500 words from books, 250 words from articles or journals, and any number of lines of poetry or lyrics from songs. There were *many* areas in the book which exceeded those limitations. So we asked Katherine for her permission to decrease the word counts if it wouldn't affect the content, or to paraphrase segments instead.

Al Hsu, Senior Editor at IVP, suggested the use of a program designed to check for uncited material in documents. We didn't want to find out later we had missed anything.

What Do You Mean We Have to Request Permission to Quote Richard's Own Words?

Once again I was just about to be hit by a wave of panic. The data we got back from the document checking program wasn't what we expected at all – there couldn't be that much uncited material remaining, could there? Picture twenty-nine pages in tiny print! I nearly lost it, considering all the citation work we had already done! Richard had been a prolific writer. We had *no idea* Richard's own words needed permissions because those versions of his words were covered by copyright law by their publishers. *Holy moly.*

So, the downsizing and paraphrasing began again in earnest. Looking back on it now, before we even met Richard and Katherine, the hand of God traced our steps. Over the years we had read as many of Richard's writings as we could, and had watched every video of his that we could find. We had attended NAIITS symposiums and listened to him speak. At those symposiums we often ended up in the same talking circles and during workshops had conversations there, in the Wiconi information booth, at Wiconi Family Camp and Powwow, by email, and at gatherings with friends.

Most of the topics of conversation related to his views on Native American contextual ministry and current events in Indian Country. Ray and I had a basic working knowledge of contextual ministry because of our conversations with him and our other friends. We use what we learned from them in our own local outreach to the Native communities near us, and on other reservations in our state. I use the concepts of contextual ministry while serving Indigenous clients at the clinic where I work.

Earlier in my life, I had the benefit of exposure to theological concepts through my Dad and his work as Department Chair in a Christian college. That helped me immensely when copyediting a theological document such as Richard's dissertation.

So, when we needed to downsize or paraphrase, we would pray, and Holy Spirit would bring back memories of past instruction, readings, videos, or personal or email conversations. Almost every time we were clearly prompted to remember what Richard had said about various topics in the book.

All the citations, rewrites, and paraphrases were completed one step at a time. The challenge was at first daunting, but then progressed to exhilarating. We knew we were doing what we were designed to do – and were created to do together as a couple! Our dream was coming to fruition.

Are We There Yet?

Not quite! It isn't over 'til it's over'. We wanted a full bibliography and inputted all the sources cited – but also included books Richard simply mentioned as helpful. If *we* gained most of our early Native American contextual ministry education by reading the books in Richard's endnotes for *One Church, Many Tribes* and the bibliographies in Randy Woodley's books, might Holy Spirit lead some *other people* called into the 'dream' of Native American ministry to do the same with the bibliographical entries in the *Cowboys* book? Maybe so. We hope so!

What about discussion questions? Might they also prompt students to study further? After Richard's passing, his personal assistant had told us that Richard said he intended to put discussion questions at the end of each chapter, to help both students and professors. Richard once told me that he was surprised (I wasn't!) that *One Church, Many Tribes* was being used as a seminary textbook, intimating that he hoped the *Cowboys* book would be as well – and that has happened. So, Ray (who had taught at a community college) and I set out to put questions at the end of each chapter. But how do you do that without the author's help, while still staying true to his 'voice'?

I can't even begin to tell you how many times during the editing process that Ray and I asked each other, 'What would Richard want?' We asked that question about the discussion questions and prayed again.

We remembered, or were reminded by Holy Spirit, that there was a section in Richard's dissertation called 'Questions Worth Asking'. We went over that list of questions and cut and pasted them at the end of their corresponding chapters. But we needed several more. Some we took from within the chapters themselves where Richard had actually posed questions for thought. We still needed more, so we looked into the chapters for what we knew to be Richard's 'hot topics'. We used his own words to the best of our ability and merged them with memories of our conversations with him to form the few needed remaining questions.

Not far into this process, we were contacted by the editor for the NAIITS journals. She said that Richard's last academic paper, 'Rescuing Theology from the Cowboys' was published in the 2012 NAIITS journal. Richard had presented the paper at that symposium. On behalf of NAIITS, she offered an excerpt of that paper to be used as an appendix to the book.

After *months* of work with InterVarsity, we had only four more days to get the assignments completed, the text polished, and the manuscript sent back to them. Then 'disaster' struck. Ray fell and broke his right arm badly, requiring surgery – two metal plates and a bone graft, not to mention time in the hospital! Can you say, 'spiritual warfare'? The Wiconi prayer warriors were alerted again. InterVarsity graciously gave us an extension.

Can You Judge a Book By Its Cover?

As we got closer to the finish line, we got another email from IVP – this time about artwork for the cover of the book. Again we wondered, 'What would Richard want?' IVP's design team submitted four initial designs for Katherine's review. IVP's artists considered the theme of the book and integrated Native American-style artwork. They were all beautifully and thoughtfully designed. Katherine asked for our opinions and those of other friends and family members.

The bottom line was, as professionally crafted as they were, none of them stood out as being the 'right one'. So, 'back to the old drawing board!' IVP took the input from Katherine, the others, and us under consideration. They returned two more suggestions using the image 'Lakota Trinity', which we had submitted for consideration. The one Katherine chose became the cover for *Rescuing the Gospel from the Cowboys*. Not only did this version reflect Richard's Lakota heritage, but we knew that he had admired Fr. John Giuliani's artwork. Many friends have since said how strikingly beautiful the cover is. We agree.

And There's More!

Richard had included a preface, but had not indicated whom he might have considered to write a foreword. We spent time in discussion with

Katherine over this. The underlying impetus was to have the entire book 'Native from cover to cover'.

Well then, what about the foreword? It makes sense to invite a known author or, in this case, a well-known theologian to write a foreword to attract as many readers as possible. We thought IVP might suggest such choices – but we wanted to honor Richard with a Native author for the foreword. Katherine said Richard would have had trouble choosing just one person – he loved and respected all his friends and academic colleagues. I suggested that the foreword could be jointly written by four of Richard's closest friends. Katherine agreed and we believed this to be Holy Spirit's guidance. So, Ray and I contacted Randy Woodley, PhD, (Keetoowah descendant); Terry LeBlanc, PhD, (Gitpu), Mi'kmaq/Acadian, Listuguj First Nation/Campbellton; Ray Aldred, (Neyihaw), Cree; and Adrian Jacobs (Ganosono), Turtle Clan, Cayuga Nation, Six Nations Haudenosaunee Confederacy. They generously offered to help and we contacted Al with Katherine's request. To our great delight InterVarsity agreed.

Our friends crafted an exceptional and heart-felt foreword with Terry directing as well as writing. To the best of our knowledge, *Cowboys* is the only book in existence with a foreword jointly written by four Native American/First Nations theologians. In addition to that, Adrian Jacob's haunting poem, 'You Just Ghosted,' was included at Katherine's request.[3]

Has it Really Been a Year Already?

Well – almost! After all the work, grieving, exhilaration, and long nights in front of the computer, the completion and simultaneous 'birth' of the *Cowboys* book was accomplished!

Can't you see the hand of God in this entire process – this continuing journey? Psalm 139 indicates that he is acquainted with all our ways and traces our paths. He knew us before we were born and his thoughts for us are endless.

When our calling into Native American ministry was confirmed in 2007, we wondered where we would end up. We thought perhaps

---

[3] Adrian Jacobs has also authored *Aboriginal Christianity: The Way It Was Meant to Be* (self-published, 1998), *Pagan Prophets and Heathen Believers: Native American Believers in the God of the Bible* (self-published, 1999), and a book of poetry, *Sacred Clowns* (self-published, n.d.). Dr Woodley's books are listed in the bibliography.

he would call us to serve on a reservation as missionaries. We travelled to nearby reservations and attended powwows and festivals in order to seek out friendships. We still do. I networked with tribal healthcare clinics and a tribal community wellness program through my work at the clinic and Wiconi connections.

Little did we know or expect that our calling to Native ministry would be through the written word – through publishing and academics. After *Cowboys,* we began working with Dr Casey Church (Potawatomi) on his dissertation which became the book, *Holy Smoke: The Contextual Use of Native American Ritual and Ceremony. Holy Smoke* outlines the process of using Native American ceremonies in Christ-honoring ways to help in the process of 'restoration of souls,' effective alcohol rehabilitation, and salvation through Creator's son Jesus.[4]

Back to the Bins

After finishing the editing work on *Holy Smoke,* we 'dove back' into Richard's bins! It had taken about a year to transform the sermons and other documents into digital format. What a blessed education we got – we weren't just typing and editing, we were being saturated with scripture as we read. We felt like we were getting portions of a free seminary education! But there was *so* much material! What to choose for the next book?

What if There Are to be Two Stories in One Book?

Richard had said he eventually wanted to write another 'popular read'. We have been granted an *amazing* story – one straight from our Creator. What if our story could be braided together with Richard and Katherine's like Terry, Randy, Ray, and Adrian's had been woven together as the foreword for *Cowboys?*

The National Park Inn

Ray and I went to the National Park Inn near Mt. Rainier ('Tacobet' – per local Pacific Northwest Natives) for a late fall weekend away in November 2015. We wanted a beautiful setting without distractions to seek the Lord about how to go about writing *this* book – and how to include some of Richard's sermons in it.

We got to the lodge and a deluge began! Ray suddenly came down with a 'monster' cold and took cold tablets that allowed him to sleep most of the night and the next afternoon. The lodge is rustic and

---

[4] Church, *Holy Smoke.*

there is no television, WiFi, or phone reception (except for a pay-phone in the lobby).

As Ray rested, I asked the Lord for wisdom and understanding. I picked up a pen and a spiral notebook and began brainstorming, sorting through sermons, and writing down ideas. It seemed possible that both a 'popular read' and an anthology of Richard's sermons could happen eventually. As I wrote, I sensed the guidance of Holy Spirit – the 'anointing' hit me. I wrote non-stop for nearly three hours, completing what would be the first and second chapters of this book.

It also occurred to me that while Ray and I were progressing to the fruition of God's dream for our lives, so had Richard and Katherine. Then their journey intersected with and ignited ours! So, why not a story of our combined journeys – our continuing journeys of following our God-given dreams?

The Conclusion – or is it Our Continuing Story?

But just where does our story end – or does it? Richard's journey continues on the other side of the 'veil' – but his words continue to impact and change the means of ministry to and by the next generations. How do we continue on this journey and effectively pass on the 'baton' to the next generation? As written words have been placed within our grasp, we pray that those words be anointed and that we have beautiful feet – the feet of those who bring good news (Rom. 10.15). Our Creator's son Jesus had the most beautiful feet to ever walk here on earth – talk about good news!

What do we (Ray and I) have to offer to continue the spread of the good news of the gospel, to increase the effectiveness of spreading the gospel to Indigenous people everywhere? In and of ourselves, nothing. We are nothing but for the unexpected, surprising grace of God.

But he *has* given us a story – a story of two white people with minimal amounts of Native DNA, shocked by an undeserved call from God, having a stretching, challenging education in Native American history and missions. We had to start from 'square one'. We were scared, intimidated, and blessed overwhelmingly.

We are often asked questions by our own friends and relations, both young and old. They want to know about Wiconi, NAIITS, and Native American contextual ministry – and about Native American people in general. We do not consider ourselves experts about Native Americans or Native American ministry, but we do know more than when we started, and we are blessed to have many friends to help us. If we can be a bridge between cultures to work together in the Body of Christ, we consider ourselves greatly privileged.

The next generation of people called into Native ministry is also asking questions. They often want to know, 'Why hasn't the previous style of ministry been more effective in sharing the gospel with Native people?' It is the same question Richard and Katherine and our other Native contextual friends began asking all those years ago. They cleared the path – they prepared the way for the next generations. We realize they are human beings like the rest of us. We have sometimes seen their tears, witnessed their outbursts of anger at injustices, and heard their passionate songs. And we danced our prayers along with them. We see lives changed – and we have seen our own lives changed in a good way!

Join us on our journey – make the choice to follow your call from God and press through in spite of opposition, criticism, and sometimes the apparent death of your dream. Holy Spirit is waiting to use you to change the world!

Discussion Questions

1. Discuss ways you can educate yourself (or pursue an education) if called into a field for which you are not prepared or educated.

2. Sometimes Christian friends or family members will tell you that you should continue in a profession you had previously trained for. How do find the balance between respecting godly counsel and following Holy Spirit's leading into something new?

3. How do you develop a network of like-minded Christian friends to support you with prayer on your journey?

PART 2

Passing the Torch of Native American Contextual Ministry to the Next Generation

One generation shall praise Your works to another,
and shall declare Your mighty acts (Ps. 145.4, NKJV).

6

WAS EVERYTHING WE WERE EVER TAUGHT ABOUT NATIVE AMERICAN CULTURE AND MINISTRY WRONG?

> **Intergenerational Ministry**
> There are progressive young people with a vision for reaching their peers. There is an older generation with a vision to reach the lost. Can both generations walk together hand-in-hand under the rule and reign of Jesus Christ, the King of Kings? They may have different opinions concerning doctrine, church traditions, and structures. They may differ in appearance, style, and choice of worship music.
>
> The challenge is, can we break past the barriers that keep us focused on ourselves and avoid the attitudes that cause division? *The Spirit of the Lord is saying it is time.*[1]

As a child I was taught – backed up by appropriate scriptural teaching – to avoid the things of the occult. All those years of conservative protestant thought I was raised with – though not taught from the pulpit as I recall – also included negative comments about Native American beliefs. This teaching was delivered via youth group study topics, recommended reading, and tracts about the 'evils' of the occult – which in their opinion included Native American religion, traditions, and stories. This teaching was 'burned into my brain' from childhood on. I recall Native Americans being accused of idolatry, nature worship, pantheism, and syncretism.

---

[1] Richard Twiss, 'A Prophetic Church' (sermon presented at New Discovery Community Church, Vancouver, WA, July 10,1994).

I don't remember ever being taught anything positive about Native American spiritual beliefs. There was no mention of devotion to our Creator-God, high regard for caring for your community, or the traditional Native respect for all of creation and our connection with it.

Guilt and Rage-producing Enlightenment

I remember very little about the Pennsylvania history class I was required to complete as a high school requirement. I do remember the teacher telling us, 'We could be proud because William Penn was good to the Indians, and Pennsylvania had never had an Indian war'. I don't think Native American history was discussed at all except for that.

After being called to serve Native people, Ray and I began to be greatly disturbed by facts we were discovering. It seems that the first Indian boarding school was in Carlisle, Pennsylvania. From the late 1800s through the early 1900s, thousands of Native children were removed from their homes and sent to either government or church boarding schools to 'Kill the Indian and save the man' – to force assimilation and 'make them white'.[2] There had been no mention of this in my history class – I would have remembered.

I began to feel both guilt and rage building up in me to near-explosive levels. The more I read, the angrier I became – guilt over my own European heritage and how my own European-immigrant relatives had treated the local Natives – and rage at the perception of being 'deceived'. I know my Pennsylvania history teacher was using the book with which she had been provided. I don't believe she was deliberately lying to the class – I just don't think she knew the truth. I really don't think anyone I was connected with knew anything much about Native Americans at all. There are no Indian reservations in Pennsylvania, and if any Native Americans were among my classmates, they were invisible to us.

---

[2] Richard H. Pratt, 'Official Report of the Nineteenth Annual Conference of Charities and Correction, 1892', pp. 46-59. Reprinted in Richard H. Pratt, 'The Advantages of Mingling Indians with Whites', in F.P. Prucha (ed.), *Americanizing the American Indians: Writings by the 'Friends of the Indian' 1880-1900* (Cambridge, MA: Harvard University Press, 1973), pp. 260-71.

You Need to Know Who You Really Are

I am a person of mixed European descent. My Mom's family heritage is mostly German from towns in Bavaria and Alsace-Lorraine. My Dad's family is English, German, Dutch, Irish, and a little French. My Dad's family oral tradition says there was a Leni Lenape (Delaware) Indigenous woman in the family in the mid-1700s. In each generation since then, someone has had black or very dark brown hair, dark skin and dark eyes. In my generation, my brother and I have the very dark hair and complexion. According to the family story, racism caused my ancestor and his Lenape wife to be erased from the family Bible and will.

Who am I Anyway?

I think most of us go through times of soul-searching – times of wondering who we are, who God made us to be, and how we fit into the world. As a Christian definitely called by God to serve Native American people, who am I and how do I fit into this new group of Native friends? Why didn't God call me when I was younger? All of these questions swirled around in my head until I was too dizzy to maintain spiritual balance.

My Mom gave me some wise advice. She told me I was out of balance and needed to have fun spending time with family and friends and doing things I enjoyed, to counteract the overwhelming negative emotions produced by what we were reading. I was so intent on following God's leading and learning about Native American culture and history, I went overboard and nearly burned myself out. Mom was right. I began getting out of the house for some fresh air on a regular basis, resumed watercolor painting, watched comedy films, and went to the beach with Ray. We also went away for short 'vacations' on weekends. First and foremost, it was necessary to spend quiet time in prayer and Bible study on a regular basis.

Early on in our journey, I remember having a very self-focused 'pity party'. I was lamenting the fact that God called 'me' into Native American ministry at the age of fifty – why didn't you call me when I was twenty? I could have done so much more for you! I felt too old (and scared) to 'start over' with something absolutely unfamiliar to me. I was really getting into it – into myself! You know how sometimes Holy Spirit speaks in a 'still, small, voice'? *Not this time.* Deep in my heart, I heard him *loudly* and clearly say, 'I knew how old you were when I called you'. Slap. Wakeup call. It isn't all about me. It's about what God wants to do and the people he intends to bless. Moses was eighty when he got started, right?

Thoughts on the Journey to Contextual Ministry

When you are going through a state of transition and introspection you can become stretched to the 'spiritual max'. I/we began to re-think what we had been taught in the past. Joshua 1.8 says, 'Keep this Book of the Law always on your lips; meditate on it day and night, so that you may be careful to do everything written in it. Then you will be prosperous and successful.' The obvious answer to all our questions about what we had been taught would be in the scriptures – we needed to meditate on the scriptures and compare them to what we were learning about Native spirituality and Native American con-textual ministry.

We don't know everything there is to know about what we have observed, but here are some of the thoughts we pondered and searched the scriptures over:

Who Gets to Decide How Much of the Bible is Literal and How Much is Symbolic?

We believe in the literal death and resurrection of our Lord Jesus Christ. It is not symbolic; we know it is real. I began wondering about theological concepts such as symbology.

In the Old Testament, Balaam's donkey was given the ability to speak; it was not symbolic, it was real. (Num. 22.30). Neither Adam nor Eve seemed to be surprised when the serpent spoke to them in the garden. St. Francis of Assisi is noted for his communication with God's creation. How many of *us* have talked to our dog or cat?

There are times in scripture when it is possible for elements of crea-tion to listen and obey – in reality, not symbolically. Jesus spoke to a fig tree and it died. In the same section of Scripture he said, 'Truly I tell you, if anyone says to this mountain, "Go, throw yourself into the sea," and does not doubt in their heart but believes that what they say will happen, it will be done for them' (Mk. 11.22-25). Jesus also spoke to the wind. 'He got up, rebuked the wind and said to the waves, "Quiet! Be still"! Then the wind died down and it was com-pletely calm' (Mk 4.39).

Sometimes God gives human beings the ability to speak to creation as well. Joshua did. 'On the day the Lord gave the Amorites over to Israel, Joshua said to the Lord in the presence of Israel: 'Sun, stand still over Gibeon, and you, moon, over the Valley of Aijalon' (Josh.10.12). It did stand still!

Some Native Americans seem to have the ability to speak with animals and plants. Are we sure this is not a truly God-given gift?

Thoughts about Creation

Dr Randy Woodley's *Shalom and the Community of Creation: An Indigenous Vision* got our attention. He posits that Native American thought about creation is much like Old Testament Hebrew belief about the 'community of creation'. He also goes into detail about the Native American concept of 'harmony' and effectively connects it with the Hebrew concept of Shalom.[3] Randy and his wife are champions of godly environmental stewardship.

The Use of Incense in Prayer

Our Native American friends often pray using incense – sage, cedar, or sweet grass – in smudging rituals and pipe ceremonies.[4] Our contextual Native Christian friends use these ceremonies in Christ-honoring ways. Ezekiel was commanded by the Lord to prophesy to the four winds (Ezek. 37.9). Jesus spoke to the winds and they obeyed. During a pipe ceremony, it is customary to pray toward the four (sometimes six) directions acknowledging God's presence in every direction.[5] Sound familiar?

In the book of Leviticus, the Jewish people were directed to celebrate the Feast of Tabernacles. 'On the first day you are to take branches from luxuriant trees – from palms, willows and other leafy trees – and rejoice before the Lord your God for seven days' (Lev. 23.40).

To this day, there are Jewish people who wave the branches toward six directions. 'With these four species in hand, one recites a blessing and waves the species in all six directions (east, south, west, north, up and down), symbolizing the fact that G-d is everywhere'.[6]

---

[3] Randy Woodley, *Shalom and the Community of Creation: An Indigenous Vision* (Grand Rapids, MI: Eerdmans Publishing Company, 2012).

[4] Church, *Holy Smoke*, p. 61.

[5] Church, *Holy Smoke*, pp. 81-83.

[6] Tracey Rich, 'Sukkot'. http://jewfaq.org/index.shtml. Accessed Oct. 27, 2016.

The Jewish, Catholic, and Orthodox traditions still use incense in prayer. Scripture includes the 'recipes' for incense used in the Jewish temple. 'Then the Lord said to Moses, "Take fragrant spices – gum resin, onycha and galbanum – and pure frankincense, all in equal amounts, and make a fragrant blend of incense, the work of a perfumer. It is to be salted and pure and sacred. Grind some of it to powder and place it in front of the Ark of the Covenant law in the tent of meeting, where I will meet with you. It shall be most holy to you"' (Exod. 30.34-36).

Angelic Beings Don't Always Appear Human

> Their faces looked like this: Each of the four had the face of a human being, and on the right side each had the face of a lion, and on the left the face of an ox; each also had the face of an eagle. Such were their faces. They each had two wings spreading out upward, each wing touching that of the creature on either side; and each had two other wings covering its body (Ezek. 1.10-11).

Many Indigenous tribes have legends about 'beings' sent by Creator to help them in times of crisis. For example, the Native people of the Pacific Northwest have legends about 'Thunderbird' being sent to help them on such occasions.[7]

Are we so sure that there is no truth whatsoever in any one of these stories? We know guardian angels exist – and not all 'angelic beings' appear human.

I don't know and I don't understand all of Native American spiritual teaching. I can't possibly claim to comprehend all there is to know about God or the Holy Scriptures. What I am saying is that rather than lumping all Native American spiritual thought into a box labelled 'demonic', we should study the practices and beliefs in light of the scriptures, and pray for Holy Spirit's guidance.

There is a *vast* difference between respect and worship. The majority of Native people we have met or consider friends *respect*, rather than *worship* creation.

---

[7] This information came from a conversation I had with an elder from one of the Pacific Northwest tribes.

How do you 'Switch' to Ministry in a Contextual Way?

Ray and I read all we could about Native American contextual ministry from the time of our clear calling. We learned that traditionally, our Native brothers and sisters are far more community-minded than our white relations. I was raised to be independent, self-supporting, and nuclear family-supporting – very much a white, protestant, capitalist seeking to take care of myself and my own family. We began to see that – from a traditional tribal people's perspective – relationship and taking care of *all* their relations, including all of creation, far surpasses the importance of 'self'. The 'we' is far more important than the 'me'.[8]

I found this a difficult concept to comprehend, given my own cultural upbringing. I do not believe either is 'right' or 'wrong', but they are certainly different. I started searching the scriptures for God's idea of how a Christian community should look. I saw the early Christians sharing all they had and supporting one another, which sounds much like Native American tradition. I admit that for years previously I had sensed an internal longing for extended community but had no concept that others actually lived that way.

When we allow Holy Spirit to 'renew our minds' through the study of scripture and his influence in our lives (Rom. 12.2), it is possible to have your mind 'rewired' in a way that causes progress toward thinking as Christ does (having the mind of Christ).

I would like to submit that contextual ministry is like learning another language – albeit a 'cultural' language. I once talked with Richard Twiss about the need for culturally bilingual people in ministry – people who are 'bridges' between cultures, working together in ministry. 'If a person wants to communicate the good news of Jesus Christ, he must become a cultural insider, learn the cognitive structure and values of the receptor culture, and so enter the culture's experiential world.'[9]

I believe this is what Paul was describing in Rom. 12.2. Richard said that Paul was a contextual minister, and that Paul's claim to 'be all things to all people in order that I might win some', was rooted in

---

[8] Twiss, *One Church, Many Tribes*, p. 99.
[9] Richard Twiss, 'North American Native Worldview' (sermon presented to New Discovery Community Church, Vancouver, WA, 1994).

his own ability to move back and forth between different cultural settings'.[10] If this is God's 'protocol', why not dive into contextual ministry? Why not be 'bridge people'?

In order to do this, Ray and I began to attend and volunteer at Native American festivals and powwows in the Vancouver, Washington, area with our Wiconi friends – and of course at the Wiconi Family Camp/Powwow. We also made a point of attending Native events, festivals, and powwows close to where we live.

I can't really say the non-Christian Native events and gatherings are 'secular'. They are not. All areas of life are considered sacred to Native Americans – there is no separation between sacred and secular for them.[11] Richard said that some traditional powwow dances are prayers. In the past nine years, we have not met even one Native person who does not have a deep respect for Creator-God. We have found them to be prayerful and spiritual people.

In every culture, there are people who worship created beings or objects. No doubt there are those in Native cultures who do, or have in the past. I suspect some of my pre-Christian Celtic ancestors worshipped aspects of or objects of creation in some way. *We are all in it together if we look back far enough*, regardless of our cultural heritage.

A Question of Trust

Many books have been written about the atrocities levelled against Native people. Dee Brown's *Bury My Heart at Wounded Knee* is one of them; it is a difficult but important book to read.[12] Much of what we have read or watched in films has been very hard to take. We were absolutely shocked to find out that some Native people who are now friends still do not have indoor plumbing or electricity in their homes on their reservations. It took me a while to believe this is actually true in our country. We know that issues of racism exist even now. With such a history, is it any wonder that many Native Americans hesitate to trust those from our Anglo society?

I remember sitting across the table at the Chinese restaurant with Richard and Randy at our first dinner together. They were gracious

---

[10] Twiss, *Rescuing the Gospel from the Cowboys*, p. 201.

[11] Twiss, *Rescuing the Gospel from the Cowboys*, p. 91.

[12] Dee Brown, *Bury My Heart at Wounded Knee: An Indian History of the American West* (New York: Holt, Rinehart & Winston, 1970).

and polite, but I was nervous. This was maybe the second or third time we had sought friendship – and perhaps a ministry connection – with Native Americans.

We did have a Native family we had become close friends with locally. Our kids went to school together. We appreciate Charley Sloan-Tso and her family for offering trust, being willing to teach us, and for choosing to speak their Navajo language in front of us at times so we could hear something precious and rare. Until 2007, I had known nothing more about Native people than what I had seen in John Wayne movies, and then later, 'Dances with Wolves'.[13] Ray and I read Richard and Randy's books – and those listed in their endnotes and bibliographies in order to educate ourselves.[14]

We so appreciate the friendships (and trust) offered to us by our Wiconi International and NAIITS (North American Institute for Indigenous Theological Studies: An Indigenous Learning Commun-ity) friends. We consider them 'family'. We also value the friendships we have made with Native people closer to our home. Some are traditional, some are Jesus-followers. All are dear to us.

However long it took for trust and friendship to develop, we are richer for it. In our Anglo society, friendships can develop quickly – we always seem to be in a hurry. I tend to be that way. I think maybe taking more time is wiser.

I remember Richard asking us at our first dinner together, 'How do you know God has called you into Native ministry?' This is a valid question for anyone called into ministry with any people group. I now know that Richard had previously encountered many people who believed they were called into Native ministry and, after a while, quit and went away. Perhaps they were called but became discouraged. Maybe they had heard a stirring appeal at a missions conference. No matter what your calling from God, it won't be easy – but it is worth taking the risk and making the choice. If you are truly following

---

[13] Michael Blake, 'Dances with Wolves', Feature film, Directed by Kevin Costner (Los Angeles, CA: MGM Studios, 1990).

[14] Twiss, *One Church, Many Tribes*; Randy Woodley, *Living in Color: Embracing God's Passion for Ethnic Diversity* (Downers Grove, IL: InterVarsity Press, 2004); and Randy Woodley, *Mixed Blood, Not Mixed Up: Finding God-given Identity in a Multi-cultural World* (Scotland, PA: Healing the Land Publishing, 2005).

God's best plan for your life, you have the power of Holy Spirit behind you – the power of the resurrection to change the world. I want in!

Discussion Questions

1. Describe your own cultural, educational, or denominational biases.

2. We should not immediately accept or reject cultural traditions and ceremonies. How do you find answers to your own questions concerning unfamiliar worship styles or traditions?

3. How have you found balance when surprised by injustices?

7

NAVIGATING NATIVE CULTURE AS A CONTINUING LEARNING PROCESS

I admit that in my cultural ignorance of my Native brothers and sisters I expected them to be just like white Americans – only darker. After all, we all live in the same country – or maybe in Canada! What a shock to my Anglo background to discover that Native culture was vastly unfamiliar to me. Ray and I had been stationed overseas while in active military service. We know what it is like to live in a culture foreign to us. We were surprised that the Native people we had met in ministry and in our local area were every bit as culturally unique as the people in the European countries we had lived in.

We began to suspect – actually we were sure – that we were in for an amazing learning process. We understood that there was *absolutely no way* we could possibly learn every cultural aspect of every tribe. You probably can't either. So, we hope it will be helpful to share a bit of what we've learned.

Cultural Diplomacy

Photography
In Native American tradition, it is a breach of protocol to take photos or video of people dressed in their regalia (traditional dress), or while performing certain ceremonies, dances, or drum songs without first asking their permission. This is true even when far away and using a high-powered long-distance camera lens. Sometimes these events, songs, or dances are forms of prayer to our Creator.

The importance and sacred nature of regalia was previously un-known to us. It is fairly common for 'powwow' protocol to be an-nounced at the beginning of the venue over the loudspeaker or printed on flyers. Some cultural outsiders ignore the rules (or are just ignorant of them) and take the photos anyway.[1]

One year Ray and I attended the Native American Youth and Family Center, Portland, Oregon (NAYA), powwow and visited our Wiconi friends. At the time we were thinking about moving to the Vancouver, Washington, area to become more actively involved with Wiconi. We had learned as much as we could about Native American culture, but due to the distance we didn't know our friends as well as we wanted to. We visited as often as we could.

Richard was planning to dance in this powwow and was serving on NAYA's board of directors at the time. He was a very tall, impos-ing man and appeared even taller and *more* imposing when wearing his colorful regalia and his 'roach' (a feather dance headdress).

We had been wondering if we could work with Richard on a more regular basis as volunteers. We knew him to be a godly man and had learned much from him – but could we fully trust him? The problem wasn't him, it was me. I didn't trust myself not to make some stupid cultural blunder. I wondered if we could trust him not to 'slam' us if we screwed up and did something incredibly, culturally stupid with-out thinking.

As Ray and I were talking with friends at the NAYA powwow, Richard was standing about six feet from us. A pushy white tourist with a camera ran over to Richard, put his arm around him and said, 'You don't mind if I get a picture with you, do you?' – obviously intending to get the photo regardless of the answer. Richard just smiled and allowed it without comment. The friend we were talking with said, 'Another of our friends would have said something about that'. I said, 'That's what grace is for'.

At that precise moment I knew in my heart that we could trust Richard to extend grace to us if we acted like human beings and made cultural, or any other kind of mistakes.

---

[1] Richard Twiss gave a talk about such protocols before our first Wiconi Family Camp and Powwow in 2009. We also learned from printed instructions distributed during the Seafair powwow in Seattle, Washington in 2009, and from Dr Casey Church.

The Concept of Generosity

We have been told that the measure of wealth in Native American society is how much one can give away – not how much can be accumulated in life.[2] An excellent example of this focus was placed in front of us early in our contextual walk when we attended a potlatch – a traditional Native American feast where many gifts are given to the attendees. This potlatch was a Christian function at a church on a nearby reservation.

We really didn't know what to expect, but a few of our Wiconi friends were in the crowd of perhaps four hundred people. The music was provided by our friend Jerry Chapman, Drumspeaker to the Nations,[3] among others. Jerry and his wife Leslie have a prophetic music ministry (using Native drums) in Washington State. There were other excellent musicians, teachers, preachers, and dancers from many tribes. Food – a *lot* of food for the whole community – is a 'given'. We feasted on dishes you would expect at a church potluck dinner, but there were traditional Native foods as well. We enjoyed the elk roast included on the menu. We were told that the elk weighed five hundred pounds and broke the axle of the pickup truck used to haul it! I also remember a particularly yummy mutton stew – a Navajo specialty.

After everyone had eaten, we assembled for the giveaway. Those sponsoring the potlatch had been gathering gifts for the potlatch for at least six months – perhaps longer. Typically, gifts are practical and include household goods, beaded jewelry, and clothing – so much that our car's trunk was filled. We learned from our Wiconi friends that to refuse the gifts (unless you had already been given the same item previously) is considered rude and should not be done.

---

[2] Charles Alexander Eastman (Ohiyesa), *The Soul of an Indian and Other Writings from Ohiyesa* (ed. Kent Nerburn; Novato, CA: New World Library, 2001), p. 28.

[3] www.jerrychapmanministries.wordpress.com/

> **Generosity**
> The original name for the Makah people (for themselves) is 'Qwee-ditch-chu-aht', which means 'people who live on the cape by the sea'. The United States government thought Makah was easier to say than *Qweeditchchuaht*.
>
> The neighboring Clallam Indians called them Makah – which means 'generous with food'. They were known for their generosity. They had a reputation among their neighbors in the Puget Sound area for being generous with their resources – their traditional territory is rich in sea life.
>
> The same should be said of the church of Jesus Christ – that 'they are a generous people'.[4]

Respect for Elders

It is common for an elder to be asked to say a prayer or blessing before events begin. It is protocol to stand during these prayers or during honor songs. We have learned to follow the example of the Natives in the group to know whether or not to stand.

As a traditional sign of respect, elders go through a buffet line first. If an elder wishes to speak to the people, silence and attention are expected. An elder will be given preferential seating and parking. They are traditionally treated as cultural treasures – like living libraries – and are sought out for wisdom and guidance.

We thought it was an impressive sign of generosity that elders are encouraged to take large baggies or containers for leftovers after any event that includes a meal.[5]

What is that Wonderful Smell?

Every culture has its own traditional foods and specialties. We have learned that if we are at an event of any kind where there are food vendors – to look for the booth with the longest line of locals and promptly get into it!

Being from a state without Indian reservations (Pennsylvania), I had never heard of frybread. Frybread originated as a way of using

---

[4] Richard Twiss, 'How to Enjoy Giving an Offering' (sermon presented to New Discovery Community Church, Vancouver, WA, Nov. 3, 1991).
[5] We learned this from our Wiconi friends at Wiconi Family Camp 2009 and the Chief Red Heart Memorial ceremony in Vancouver, Washington, 2014.

the sparse commodities distributed to Native Americans on reservations. The recipes vary a bit, but a reliable source (Casey) tells us that no matter who you ask, their own Mom always makes the best frybread!

In spite of its origins, frybread is delicious. It is a disk of deep fried dough sometimes topped with butter, honey, or jam. They are also the base for 'Indian tacos'. In that case, they are often topped with anything you would expect in a typical Mexican taco.

There are other cultural culinary delights such as salmon grilled on alder wood planks, shellfish cooked over heated stones and doused with seawater, authentic clam chowder in a clam-nectar base, mutton stew, roasted elk or bison, and many other specialties depending on tribe or location. Our advice is: get in that long line and enjoy!

Talking Circles

Native Americans have a tradition of discussing important issues in 'talking circles'. In our Anglo culture, the closest thing I can think of is the concept of a 'workshop' at a conference.

In a talking circle, everyone sits in a circle – no one is more important than anyone else. The person who has 'called' the circle begins the discussion and holds the 'talking stick' – or an eagle feather in some tribes. Whoever has the talking stick has 'the floor,' and no one may interrupt. When the person finishes, they pass the stick to the next person, usually to the left. This person may speak if they wish, or pass the stick to the person beside them.[6]

What's in a Handshake?

After marching behind the color guard at Wiconi Family Camp and Richard Twiss Memorial Powwow, the participating veterans are invited to stand in line near the announcer's gazebo. They are given a microphone and can then tell what their tribal affiliation is, branch of service, if they served in combat, and so on. Then the dancers who have followed behind during grand entry, and any of those in the crowd who wish to, file through and shake hands with and honor the veterans.

---

[6] We learned about talking circles both at Wiconi Family camp 2009 and the 2010 NAIITS symposium at George Fox Seminary, Newberg, Oregon, and from Dr Casey Church.

In our Anglo culture, avoiding eye contact or greeting someone with a weak handshake can be viewed as disinterest or a lack of trust. This is not true in all cultures.

At our first Wiconi powwow I wondered why the Navajo women in line to shake the veterans' hands just tapped the palm of my hand instead of shaking it. Others grasped my hand firmly and made eye contact, as I was used to in my own culture, and some seemed to have a very weak grip.

We later learned that various tribes have different protocols for greeting others. To some, eye contact and a firm shake can mean aggression. To others, avoiding eye contact is a sign of respect. A seemingly weak grip may mean 'coming in peace'. Again, it is wise to follow the lead of the Native person.[7]

Treating People with Honor

We wondered – how do we know how to approach Native people without causing offense? According to the National Congress of American Indians (NCAI), 'There are 562 federally recognized tribes in the United States'.[8] So, how should we behave in light of so many distinct tribal protocols? We were feeling more than a little overwhelmed! We learned a lot from an Apache elder who taught a workshop on protocol at our first Wiconi Family Camp.

We also read quite a bit about cultural protocol in books listed in the bibliographies we had been sorting through for resources. One of the best books we have read for protocol guidance is *Warfare by Honor: The Restoration of Honor: A Protocol Handbook* by Qaumaniq and Dr Iglahliq Suuqiina.[9]

---

[7] We learned this from Navajo friends and Dr Casey Church.

[8] National Congress of American Indians, 'Indian Nations in the United States', www.ncai.org/about-tribes/indians_101.pdf, p. 12. Accessed Aug. 20, 2017.

[9] Qaumaniq Suuqiina and Iglahliq Suuqiina, *Warfare by Honor: The Restoration of Honor: A Protocol Handbook* (Scotland, PA: Healing the Land Publishing, 2007).

> ## The Spirit World
> At one meal I sat with men from Samoa, New Zealand, Mozambique, and the Solomon Islands. They spoke of how in their respective cultures the ideas of spiritual warfare and territorial spirits were not just theological ideologies but were daily spiritual realities and occurrences.
>
> They chuckled at the thought of some of these issues causing a concern in theological circles in the United States. The idea of warring in prayer and intercession against these things *not* being biblical was for them absurd, as we well know being from a Native culture.
>
> For us, spirits and demonic powers are not 'possibilities' but realities that we grew up with and around.[10]

Grieving Customs

Some tribes traditionally don't mention the name of a recently deceased loved one for a year or more out of respect. If you know this is true of the people you are with, don't speak the deceased person's name. Some tribes cancel powwows or other events if there is a death in the tribe. Don't be offended if you arrive for such a function and it has been cancelled. Be respectful.[11] In some tribes it is customary to cut your hair as a sign of grief upon the loss of a loved one. For some tribes, stepping back from social events and 'laying low' in their communities is an acceptable way to grieve.[12]

Some Places are Sacred

The Jewish Temple in Jerusalem – now with only the 'Western Wall' remaining – is a sacred place to both Jewish and Christian people. There are places considered sacred in all cultures. This is true for Native American and Indigenous people. There are many tribal stories of miraculous occurrences where Creator intervened and saved people at specific locations, and these places are sometimes considered sacred. Some of these are in National or State Parks. Follow the restrictions posted when there. Some are destinations for 'pilgrimage' for Native people – for vision quests to seek Creator's guidance.

---

[10] Richard Twiss, letter to 'NANCC Guys', 6 December 1993.
[11] We were told this by Lummi friends on the Lummi Reservation in Ferndale, Washington.
[12] This information is from Dr Casey Church.

Christian people have long had traditional places of pilgrimage, and we expect them to be treated with honor.

We are taught to behave with respect when honoring our ancestors in our own Christian cemeteries. Be respectful of Native burial grounds and artifacts. There are laws covering appropriate behavior in such circumstances.

What About Sweat Lodge Ceremonies?

Sweat Lodge ceremonies are somewhat trendy these days. Many of you will have read about them on various media sources. 'New Agers' have adopted them, and anyone can find numerous online sites offering or describing sweat lodge ceremonies. There have been deaths due to inappropriate use of sweat lodges by New Age practitioners.[13] Traditionally, 'sweats' are sacred ceremonies, not *for-profit* enterprises.

Sweat lodge ceremonies have been used by Native people for generations. Most often the ceremonies are used for hygienic purposes – a 'detox' of sorts to 'sweat out' both physical and spiritual impurities. People in Scandinavian countries have been using sweat baths and saunas for centuries. It is common knowledge that working up a good sweat while running increases endorphins – the 'runner's high'. These types of physical and emotional responses can add to the benefits of the lodge experience.

If you are considering participation in a sweat lodge ceremony, why not attend one conducted by godly Christian practitioners who have been trained by their own experienced Native elders?

We knew when we became volunteers for Wiconi that 'sweats' would be offered during Wiconi Family Camp. Tribes vary in their traditions for participation in sweats. Wiconi offers sweats for men, couples, and women.

Previous teaching I had been given about the possibility of 'demonic' activity during such ceremonies made me nervous about participating – even though the ceremonies at Wiconi had been adapted for Christian worship. 'Spirits' are not invited into these Christian sweat lodge ceremonies – only the Holy Spirit is welcomed, creating a safe place for prayer and healing. I was extremely curious about the Christian contextual use of the Sweat Lodge Ceremony. I knew the

---

[13] Felicia Fonseca, 'Author Convicted in Ariz. Sweat Lodge Deaths Freed', NBC News July 12, 2013, nbcnews.com/news/other/author-convicted-ariz-sweat-lodge-deaths-freed-f6C10620484. Accessed May 13, 2017.

temperature experienced in a sweat would be *intensely* hot. I found out later that there are various levels of heat settings ranging from beginner to experienced.[14]

I chose to attend the Wiconi 'ladies sweat' during the 2009 Wiconi Family Camp. The truth is, part of my motivation was to check it out for 'appropriateness' in Christian worship. Even so, underlying or perhaps overriding my 'scientific objectivity' as a nurse, was a nagging question in the back of my mind: 'What if there is something I can learn about God that I can't find out any other way?' I want more of God. I want as much of him as he knows I can handle with his help. Then I want him to expand my capacity so I can learn more of his 'ways' and contain even more of him!

I decided to participate in spite of my fears and was determined to 'stick it out' to the end of the ceremony – I didn't want to miss anything. What if a new insight into our Lord's 'ways' was to be revealed to me late in the ceremony?

Wiconi sweats actually begin before the ceremony itself – with prayer. There is a protocol set down by trained practitioners. The leader of the sweat teaches about the ceremony and its protocol before the sweat lodge is entered. The lodge is traditionally constructed of natural material. The sweat lodges at Wiconi Family Camp are made of PVC pipes overlaid with tarps. As Casey explained to us, it is not about what the structure is made of – it is about the prayers said inside the sweat lodge. Western-style churches (houses of prayer) are constructed from a variety of materials as well.[15]

Modesty is important. Men are asked to wear shorts, and if they wish, they can wear t-shirts. Women are asked to wear a 'sweat dress,' which is made specifically for the occasion. If they don't have a sweat dress, they are asked to wear shorts, a loose-fitting t-shirt, and bring a towel to cover their legs. This is a prayer meeting – a place for meeting with our Creator-God through his son Jesus.[16] We were cautioned to remove jewelry, watches, wire-rimmed glasses, and any other metal items because they would become very hot inside the lodge.

Those who were first-timers, the elderly, or anyone who had health concerns were encouraged to be close to the exit should they choose to leave before the conclusion of the ceremony. We were

---

[14] Church, *Holy Smoke*, p. 71.
[15] Church, *Holy Smoke*, pp. 57-58.
[16] Church, *Holy Smoke*, p. 58.

taught about the sacred and confidential nature of conversation, prayer, or worship occurring during the ceremony, so 'what is said in the lodge stays in the lodge'. Out of respect for the privacy of the other participants, I am only discussing my own thoughts and experiences. Some 'lodges', such as that used by the Brethren in Christ Overcomers Alcohol Treatment Program in Farmington, New Mexico, recognize that the confidential nature of the sweat lodge ceremony creates an atmosphere where cathartic release brings lasting healing.[17]

Before entering the lodge and after the teaching, we were blessed in prayer by smudging – the use of incense in worship as a symbol of purification through Christ. The leader of the sweat I attended was a Christian pastor – a Native woman with many years of experience.

About nine of us entered the lodge in a clockwise manner. Several large, round, red-hot stones were shoveled into a pit in the center of the lodge. There were 'firemen' outside tending a fire where the stones were heated until glowing.

Our leader directed us in four 'rounds' of prayer and worship. Between each round the flap was opened to allow some much-appreciated cool air to come in. The pastor poured a ladle of water from a bucket over the glowing stones to create steam. We were each offered a drink of cool water. I enjoyed the light fragrance of sage which had been placed on the hot stones. We went around the circle taking turns offering prayers or worship and sometimes a song.

As a nurse (a scientist), I am very much a 'prove it to me person'. At the same time, as a Christian believer, I was listening for Holy Spirit's voice and seeking his presence. I must say that this ceremony was the most intense prayer meeting I have ever attended – it qualifies as one of my top five Christian 'mountaintop experiences'. I have never experienced such heat – or sweated so much! The newness of the ceremony and the heat were a bit scary for my 'white' flesh! – but it was worth every bit of physical discomfort to experience – be 'saturated' with – the presence of God. I felt as if I could 'wring out' my soul and new blessings would flow out.

---

[17] The details covering the use of a contextual Christian Sweat Lodge Ceremony were provided by Dr Casey Church (Potawatomi), Director of Wiconi.

In conclusion, I will say that during the ceremony I prayed for reconciliation with relatives who had been estranged from our family for about ten years. Upon returning home, I discovered that one of those relatives had sent us an email seeking renewed communication – at the same time I had prayed that request during the sweat lodge ceremony.

God does not have to grant us confirmation – but as a 'prove it to me person,' I was greatly encouraged by that miraculous answer to my prayer.

Our Ongoing 'Conclusion'

After asking our friends and reading as much as we could (and we are *still* learning!) about tribal communities we have the closest contact with, it became obvious that we should follow the lead of the people we are with. Ask questions, but ask from the standpoint of a student – approaching with humility when you don't know how to behave or respond in certain situations. If you have the opportunity, living among and experiencing life with Native friends is a much better way to learn.

Don't expect to be able to 'learn it all'. It just isn't going to happen. Expect to make mistakes. Apologize when you should. It is likely you will be treated with grace – as we have been.

Do Your Homework
If you are going to visit a reservation or tribal function – or any people group unfamiliar to you – why not read books about them? Better still, why not look at their official tribal website beforehand? That way you will get a lesson in their history from *their* viewpoint.

To get an overview of current topics of importance in 'Indian Country' we made a habit of reading online Native news websites such as Indian Life Ministries (indianlife.org), The National Congress of American Indians (ncai.org), and Indian Country Today (no longer in operation). Indian Life Ministries produces culturally-appropriate media from a Christian viewpoint.

> **Study the Scriptures**
> As in any study of scripture for the formation of doctrine, it is important for us to know what the Bible says. We can have many opinions and many ideas about the truth, but only when we *know* that we *know* will there be power to do it – to carry it through. This can only come as we know the truth of God's word, the Bible.[18]

Pray and Search the Scriptures

Our own Western Christian ways have been influenced by our pagan roots – the use of Easter eggs being one example. If Ray and I come across Native customs, ceremonies, or traditions we don't understand, we keep in mind that God has given us all freedom of choice. We have chosen to study such traditions or concepts and ask our Native Christian brothers and sisters for their insights before automatically agreeing with or condemning what we have encountered. We go home and search the scriptures and spend time in prayer.

It is easy for human beings to immediately condemn what we don't understand. We should pray for wisdom and understanding and listen for Holy Spirit's guidance. It is also helpful to observe the practitioners for their fruit – are people being pointed to Jesus and being saved? Matthew 7.17-18 puts it well: 'Likewise, every good tree bears good fruit, but a bad tree bears bad fruit. A good tree cannot bear bad fruit, and a bad tree cannot bear good fruit'.

Parting Thoughts

Many things in life are cyclical – seasons come and go. One season can overlap another. Sometimes they switch back and forth – seem to go backwards, even. Then as one dream comes into reality, God gives us another, and another, and another. Is there really an end-goal, or is life a series of goals on a journey?

One of the last things Richard said to us was, 'The journey continues'. Why not step out into your own journey? Sometimes you just have to get out of the boat!
Amen!

---

[18] Richard Twiss, 'Kingdom Scriptures', Personal reference notes, probably 1994.

Discussion Questions

1. Have you ever visited churches of other denominations or from other cultures? If not, why not?

2. If in a place of leadership, have you invited Christian speakers including women, leaders from other denominations, races, or ethnicities to your church mission conferences? If not, why not?

3. Have you actively recruited members of those congregations to attend your conferences and assist with organizing the events if interdenominational?

AFTERWORD: MY NAME IS WRITTEN ON THE PALMS OF HIS HANDS

See, I have engraved you on the palms of my hands;
your walls are ever before me' (Isa. 49.16).

Isaiah 49.16 is my favorite Bible verse. I know it literally refers to the nation of Israel, but I take the words to heart for my own as well. Some versions say our names are 'written'; some say 'engraved'. Is it possible our names were engraved by a nail used during the crucifixion of Christ? I don't know, but there is the indication – the assurance – of permanence. Our walls *and* names are ever before his eyes.

What is a wall for? Is it protection from the elements, invaders, and a boundary we may safely work within – perhaps a 'hedge of protection' as mentioned in the book of Job?

What about engraving? Who hasn't scribbled a reminder note on their hand as a child or adult? Is it possible that our Creator has done the same to keep us 'ever before his eyes'?

He must have really big hands to hold all those engravings! How many different fonts or languages are represented in those names? Surely they are all different, reflecting the variety Creator-God placed in humanity. Yet this scripture doesn't speak in the plural, saying 'our name,' but 'my name' – seeing us all as the unique individuals we were created to be.

What a privilege to be in front of his eyes and engraved on his hands. If that's the case, doesn't he take us (our names on his hands) everywhere he goes? I wonder: Is the path, purpose, or dream for each of us there as well? I'll bet there's room!

What are hands used for? So many things! We build, eat, wash, bless, scratch our kitty's ears, scratch our own backs, write, type, cook, drive, and care for others. There is really very little we don't use our hands for.

Are we there when God's hands stretch out to administer right-eousness and justice? Our names must be, if so.

Is it possible this is one of the reasons to watch and follow what the Father is doing as Jesus did? If our name is on his hand – wouldn't it be a powerful thing to participate in what he is doing? I think so. I think his dream for us could be imbedded in the name (ours) he has engraved on his hands. I/we have chosen to follow the Father through our God-given dream.

We need to hold onto his hand – where our names are engraved – until our destined purpose ignites and fruition is the result.

Press forward to the goal. Fight the good fight. Fulfill your des-tiny. If you fall, get up and try again. If God then gives you another dream, begin again.

Know you are engraved on the palms of his hands – created for a purpose.

Sue Martell

APPENDIX A:

GOD'S PURPOSE FOR NATIVE PEOPLE

by Richard Twiss[1]

I believe a great spiritual movement will take place among the Native American people of this land. I strongly believe this will happen.

I have often wondered why God blessed our nation, the United States of America. Many have tried to find America in the Bible in order to answer this question. Why has God blessed a nation that in many cases systematically eradicated entire tribal nations of Native American people in the name of 'progress'? American history is replete with horrible and shameful acts of ethno genocide.

America is a great nation and world power. America exists because God had a purpose in mind for her. America was established by people who came to seek God. The purpose for America *was to make God known.*

As a Native American, I can say for all of us who have been chosen by God, we are grateful for God's mercy and kindness to our people. Many people today are spiritually disoriented because they dwell in darkness. 1 Peter 2.9 says, 'But you are a chosen people, a royal priesthood, a holy nation, God's special possession, that you may declare the praises of him who called you (us Indian people) out of darkness into his wonderful light'.

---

[1] Richard Twiss, 'Life with a Purpose' (excerpt from a sermon presented to New Discovery Community Church, Vancouver, WA, Aug. 30, 1992).

Native Americans did not invite the pilgrims to come to America, their villages, and hold crusade meetings and evangelistic services. They did not ask the United States Government to establish reservations for them to live on. Indian people have struggled with their identity, their loss of land, and their way of life for one hundred fifty years. They struggle with their purpose – but remember, *God has a purpose for every nation!*

I am convinced that there is a special place in the purposes of God for Native American people. They are a people who can understand what Jesus felt like when unjustly accused and persecuted, to have his human dignity stolen, to be stripped and robbed of everything he had, to be mocked by society and made a laughing stock – a people who can understand what it must have felt like for Jesus to have his father turn his back on and abandon him.

But God has a divine purpose for Native American people to fulfill. They have knowledge and gifts the church in America needs to grab hold of. Native people have a supernatural view of the world around them and of God. They have a vastly different value system when it comes to materialism and creature comforts. They know how to live very simply and in a way uncluttered by the 'American Dream'. Their security is not connected to wealth and 'things'. In their culture, they know they will always be cared and provided for.

It is my conviction that an aspect of God's purpose for Native people is to begin making a significant contribution to the body of Christ and the fulfilling of God's purposes in the earth.

APPENDIX B:

THE BLESSING OF COVENANT: NATIVE AMERICANS AND THE CHURCH

by Richard Twiss[1]

Over the years I have observed a very sad situation frustrating the genuine work of God among Native American people. What I have seen is a lack of real biblical unity and oneness among believers. It is my deep conviction and experience that an understanding and practice of covenant among God's people has the power to produce a biblical unity and relationships that truly exalt Jesus Christ, honors God the Father, and enables the Church to fulfill her mission to glorify God in all the earth.

Developing the depth and quality of unity necessary to evangelize the world, disciple the nations, and see the church grow is the primary responsibility of church leadership. It is the leader who must see the need for such relationships and then take whatever steps are needed in his or her personal life and in the church to bring them forth.

Several Potential Barriers or Points of Disunity that we Wrestle with as Native Christian People in Ministry:

- Whose definition of 'Indian' do we use?

---

[1] Richard Twiss, 'The Blessing of Covenant' (Conference presentation at Sonrise '92 International Native American Congress on Evangelism, Discipleship and Church Growth hosted by CHIEF Ministries, Mar. 9-13, 1992).

- The 'traditional' versus 'non-traditional' differences, including reservation versus urban and full-blood or mixed-blood distinctions.
- Centuries-old theological divisions in Christendom: Protestant versus Catholic, fundamental evangelicalism versus Pentecostal/charismatic, Armenian versus Calvinism positions, dispensational versus covenantal views of interpretation, and even eschatology.
- The difficult task of deciding where we draw the line in determining what is 'OK' and 'not OK' regarding cultural versus spiritual Native ceremonies and/or customs.
- The historical abuse of Christianity as a religion by the United States government in handling Native land and sovereignty issues.
- The tendency to find unity in/around racial, political, economic, or other good issues instead of God's Word and the cause of Christ.

I realize many other barriers could easily be listed, but the goal is to look at the answers and solutions to these issues and not the issues themselves.

All true believers are in covenant with God through Jesus Christ and the New Covenant, which is his blood. They are also in covenant relationship with each other. I believe that the primary influence, emphasis, and focus of our covenant in Christ should be its ability to affect lost people to know and serve God. Jesus prayed in John 17 for unity among his followers, 'That all of them may all be one,' and 'that the world may believe that you have sent me' (Jn 17.20-21). Unity, as seen in lasting relationships among Christians, is the highest form of evangelism! This great truth is expressed by Jesus himself.

As powerful as covenant is, our practice of it can never be allowed to take on an exclusive or selective effect. The word 'covenant' has received a bad connotation, sometimes justifiably so, because it was abused and became a self-serving exclusive word. It said that we and us, our church, denomination, point-of-view, was the most important thing. This attitude fosters an estranged and sequestered view toward those 'different' from us.

A Covenant-keeping God

God reveals his faithfulness and trustworthiness in that he keeps the covenant that he makes. Once God has made a covenant, he does not forget it nor become negligent of it. He always follows through with the commitments he has made. 'Know therefore that the Lord your God is God; he is the faithful God, keeping his covenant of love to a thousand generations of those who love him and keep his commandments' (Deut. 7.9).

Among Native people, giving your word was sacred. As Christians, our word should be even more trustworthy because it is based on a greater covenant. In biblical times, the word 'covenant' involved promise, commitment, faithfulness, and loyalty even unto death. A covenant was sacred and was not lightly entered into by the parties involved. In biblical times, a person was only as good as their covenant word.

Terms of the New Covenant

We are all, without exception, co-laborers with Christ and in that part of a great *team!* As important as vision is, and I don't believe anything of any real significance happens without it, covenant is the binding and unifying truth that keeps ups together as the body of Jesus Christ on earth. If the church is divided, splintered, fragmented, suspicious, jealous, or competing with others, it will never fulfill the great commission of Christ. Covenant says we must *together* go into all the world to make and teach disciples of Jesus Christ.

And Jesus Christ, the Author and Preserver of covenant, will be glorified in all the earth.

APPENDIX C:

THE NEED FOR VARIOUS STYLES OF MINISTRY

by Richard Twiss

Street Witnessing

One of my first memories of street witnessing occurred while I lived in Hawaii. I went to the market in Honolulu. There was a guy standing in center court yelling about people needing Jesus and forgiveness for their sins. He also talked about heaven, hell, and judgment. The guy seemed a little wild-eyed. He was poorly dressed. His loud, screeching voice was full of passion, anger, judgment, but also compassion. He was waving his Bible at people, doing his very best to convince them of their sin and need for Jesus as savior.

Another time at Pike Place market in Seattle, I saw a guy doing the same thing. In both cases, there were various reactions to their messages. Some scoffed, ridiculed, and yelled back. Some just laughed and shook their heads as they walked past. *Others stood to the side like me in Honolulu and listened to what he was saying – but didn't want anyone else to know they were listening* [1]

The Need for Ministry, Worship Music, and Scripture in Indigenous Languages and Styles

There are twenty million Quechua Indians in western South America. They are the descendants of the people of the Inca Empire. In five centuries of Spanish Catholic and later Protestant presence, the Bible

---

[1] Richard Twiss, 'Prepare the Way for the Lord' (sermon presented at New Discovery Community Church, Vancouver, WA, Dec. 13, 1992).

102

was never translated into the Quechua language. It is only in the last decade [as of 1992] that our brothers and sisters in Christ have God's word in their native Quechua.

When the early missionaries arrived, they made all the believers destroy their Native instruments and music in favor of European hymns, music forms, and instruments like organs, accordions, or pianos. They were told their music was of the devil.

The Quechuas have a tonal language much like the Navajo. Hymns don't work for them.

After enduring much [contextual ministry] opposition, the Quechua have begun to worship our Lord and Savior Jesus Christ using their native music. They have now written over three thousand worship songs in their language and musical style.[2]

A Growing Sense of the Potential for Contextual-style Ministry

Many ethnic people are looking for a sense of identity – a sense of where they came from. It is critically important that you know where you came from – it tells you who you are and gives you an idea of your potential.

I'm growing my hair long to begin wearing it in braids. I'm assembling a traditional dance regalia to participate at powwows – but not because I want to be like 'Kunta Kinte' from 'Roots' and find my identity in my Native culture or ancestry.

I am doing this because I believe there is a new wineskin [contextual ministry] being offered for use by the Holy Spirit in reaching Native peoples with the gospel of Christ.[3]

Take the risk and accept the challenge.
You can be effective in reaching the lost![4]

---

[2] Richard Twiss, 'Get Stirred Up' (sermon presented to New Discovery Community Church, Vancouver, WA, Mar. 15, 1992).

[3] Richard Twiss, 'Knowing Where You Came From' (sermon presented at Solid Rock Church, Feb. 14, 1993).

[4] Richard Twiss, 'Witnessing that Works' (sermon presented at New Discovery Community Church, Vancouver, WA, Mar. 25, 1990).

APPENDIX D:

THE NEED FOR LIKE-MINDED FRIENDS

by Richard Twiss

Alaska Story

Over fifteen years ago I became a Christian and member in the most life-changing small group experience I've known. I moved to Alaska to visit an old friend who was a part of the Gospel Outreach ministry. A hundred or more people lived together on a ten-acre farm in the Matanuska Valley, fifty miles north of Anchorage.

Fourteen of us single men lived in a semi-renovated chicken coop. A sense of family drew me to this lifestyle. The people had a genuine and deep level of commitment to growing up in Christ.

I grew to love deeply many of these people with which I worked, argued, prayed, and worshipped. Because our goal was to grow up in Christ, we didn't let one another continue in our sins. We challenged selfish, prideful attitudes in one another.[1]

Our God-given Need for Fellowship and Community

I believe that no Christian will ever experience his or her full spiritual growth potential without being part of a group of like-minded believers. We are not isolated individualists on an independent spiritual pilgrimage with God. We are created in God's image with a deep sense and need for fellowship. If you haven't already, surround yourself with like-minded people.

---

[1] Richard Twiss, 'Growing up in Christ' (from a sermon series presented to New Discovery Community Church, Vancouver, WA, May 13, 20, 1990).

Find those you can 'click' with – those you genuinely look forward to being with. You need to choose a group with a level of passion similar to your own. Are they ready to get down, challenge, and encourage one another with equal commitment and zeal? They must be willing to make necessary sacrifices, and 'carve out time for this thing' no matter what. They must share your dream.[2]

Surrounding Yourself with Like-minded People

I love listening to and reading about great dreamers. I've read hundreds of books by and about great dreamers, both men and women, who saw and believed God for great things – for big dreams.

I want to be inspired, challenged and encouraged to dream big. I want my children to dream big. Early on I learned that books have the power to inspire big dreams. I've read dozens and dozens of biographies about great world leaders, military leaders, and sports heroes. I've made it a point to introduce my boys to biographies of inspiring people, including those about Sitting Bull, Crazy Horse, and Chief Seattle.

If you are going to fulfill your God-given dreams, you must surround yourself with people who share in your vision from God. Sometimes it is necessary to 'change friends' in order to do this. The wrong friends can pull you down and take you in wrong directions. Their value system can be 180 degrees different from what you know you want your value system to be.[3]

The only value worth fully pursuing with all our hearts in this life is the value of knowing, loving, and serving Jesus Christ.[4]

---

[2] Twiss, 'Growing up in Christ'.
[3] Richard Twiss, 'Discovering God's Dream for Your Life' (sermon presented at New Discovery Community Church, Vancouver, WA, June 9, 1991).
[4] Twiss, 'Growing up in Christ'.

APPENDIX E:

JOURNEY TO ISRAEL, A DIARY

by Richard Twiss

House of Prayer Convocation, Historic First Year, Sept. 2-10, 1994

Friday, Sept. 2, 1994

Met 'Greg' at the [Portland, Oregon] airport. Arrived about forty-five minutes early thinking it would be sufficient for a continental flight. Didn't realize that because we were going to Israel, our check-on baggage had to be specially security checked. It took a while to check in even though we already had our tickets. We were still waiting with only fifteen minutes before the plane left. We followed the baggage guy to some gates to get checked through x-rays and missed him. After several minutes we realized we'd gone the wrong way. So we hustled our buns and finally got to our correct gate to see the loading ramp pulled away and in a moment, our plane pulling out. Our hearts sank. If we missed our TWA connection to New York, then we'd probably certainly miss the one to Israel. We hustled our buns back to the ticket counter and they scrambled to get us a seat on Northwest to Seattle which left in six minutes in order to maybe catch our TWA flight which had a one-hour layover in Seattle. Well, we hustled our now tired buns one more time and made it with ten minutes to spare and were off to New York. It was a five-hour flight to the Big Apple. We had a two-hour layover. While eating some pretzels in the terminal I looked up to be staring right at a guy that I had met in

106

Korea. What an amazing thing in that he is Samoan and still lives in Samoa. He was also heading to Israel to participate in the convocation. What a neat blessing.

It was a long ten-hour flight to Tel Aviv. As we stepped off the plane, I was hit with the heat and amazing humidity. We had arrived. Driving into Jerusalem was hard to relate to. Jerusalem, Israel! Driving from Tel Aviv from the airport to Jerusalem we drove through the valley where there were numerous abandoned army vehicles and equipment left along the hillsides to commemorate the many lives lost during the 1947-1948 War of Independence. Apparently many died trying to get food supplies through there from Tel Aviv to Jerusalem.

Our driver took us on a quick mini-tour through town. We had arrived on Shabbat (Sabbath) and everything in the Jewish sector was closed. *Everything*. The whole nation basically stops on Shabbat. Businesses, airlines, government, and so on. We drove by the old city and wall with all its gates. Damascus gate, Joppa gate. He took us up to Mt. Olivet for an awesome panoramic view of the old city with the gold-covered Dome of the Rock, West Wall, Wailing Wall, etc. It was beautiful.

We arrived at the House of Prayer ministry house on Mt. Olivet. That is where the intercessors and the logistical team for the convocation were staying. A very multinational team. Honduras, Canada, Philippines, India, USA, Israel, Czechoslovakia, Estonia, Germany, and others. Said our 'hellos' and were assigned our bunks in a men's makeshift dorm. Exactly like my old communal living days. Déjà vu!

Greg and I decided to head into the old city. We arrived at the Damascus gate and started walking. We wandered through narrow alleys with a zillion shops and stores. These were all Arab because the Jewish sector was closed. It was totally cool because these were some of the very same streets Jesus walked down. Bought some small, date treats. Very good.

It was getting dark and most of the shops were closing. Felt a little nervous. We wandered into this big courtyard of a monastery/church. Didn't find out till later, but this was the church of the Holy Sepulcher – reportedly one of two possible sites of Jesus's tomb. I was struck by the 'oldness' of everything. Big granite stones that were worn certain ways by use over time. It was a Greek Orthodox place, so all the religious folks were dressed accordingly. Black everything. It was awe-inspiring and majestic. We watched a service. Afterward we walked through the small chapel area. It was beautiful and ornately decorated.

We wandered out of the old city to catch a cab back to the House of Prayer for a hoped-for night's rest. We're on opposite time here so my body is saying it's time to start the day, but the time here says it's evening and go to bed. I can tell this will take a few days.

Sunday–
Slept in a little and we headed for a service at Christ Church in the old city. It is the oldest protestant church in the Middle East. Good group of internationals. The pastor gave a very good view of salvation and Israel in the scriptures talking about the covenants. I asked one of the ushers to ask him during a break if I could give a word of greeting and prayer request about Native Americans. I got Greg to come up with me and he said some very good words. I shared my vision for Native people and afterward many people came up and thanked us and said how encouraged they were.

Left there, and Greg, a lady from Canada, and I headed out for the city. We wandered around for several hours then made our way to the Western Wall and Wailing Wall.

When you walk into the square where the Wailing Wall is, if the women have shorts on they give them a little skirt to put on. When you go up to the Wailing Wall, the men and women are divided. They gave us little paper yarmulkes to wear on our heads or they wouldn't let us in. We prayed there for fifteen minutes and then went into a big open cavern-like place for the men. It had little library study tables and lots of guys praying, studying, and singing. Very interesting place. When Greg and I were praying at the wall a local newspaper photographer came and asked if he could take our pictures. He said they rarely ever saw Native Americans praying at the wall. It was a unique experience. I kissed the wall and interceded for God's work among Native people. These were the actual stones from Solomon's Temple. Mind boggling.

Left there and wandered around the city for several more hours. We bought a few knick-knacky things. As we were getting ready to leave the old city through the Damascus gate, we saw there were a lot of police and activity going on. We then heard the gate was closed because two guys had just been stabbed.

Most of the typical police guys are in their late teens and early twenties. They all carry Uzi or AK 47-type machine guns. Could be a little unsettling thinking these guys have to make split-second decisions – given the high tension of the political climate around here – with that fire-power. Tensions are always high between the Jews and Arabs.

It was now dark and we headed over to the new part of the city, which is Jewish. It was all new since 1967 after the Six-Day War. All very modern and sophisticated. Still many small stores and shops but very Western. Many, many young people hanging out. There are several street musicians playing. Had dinner there and caught a taxi back to the House of Prayer. Now 11.00 pm.

As we have walked around we have been the ongoing objects of people's stares and curiosity. People often turn their heads and stare as we walk by. They call us 'Red Indians' from America. Many of the Arab shop owners said things like, 'You are the real Americans. You were the first. You need to get your land back.' One fellow said that they, the Palestinians, were going to get all their land back one day. Just served to reinforce my belief again about an international openness to Native Americans.

Monday–
Greg and I visited the garden tomb. It is where the Protestants believe Jesus might have been buried. The hill they call Skull Hill, where Jesus was believed to have been crucified, looks very much like a skull. It was very neat. We spent some time praying for Indian people here.

We made it up to the gold-covered Dome of the Rock. It is an incredibly ornate and beautiful mosque. It is built over the reported site of Solomon's Temple and possibly the Ark of the Covenant. In the center is a large rock believed to be the place where Abraham offered Isaac. So much history is here. It's all very difficult to process. Here in Jerusalem you have a city viewed as a holy city to the Muslims, the Jews, and the Christians.

It was now about 2.30 and we headed back to the House of Prayer to get ready to head to the Mt. Zion Hotel where we would be staying and the conference was held.

Got checked in. I'm rooming with a guy named 'Jim'. He is the U.S. regional director for this convocation and is the ministry director for the Intercessors for America. Got settled in my room and went to dinner the first night. The Mt. Zion Hotel is a pretty nice place. Met up with several people that I'd met in Korea. A little bit of a homecoming. Worship was great as one might expect on a first night. Bill, a messianic Jew, was our worship leader. We have a worship songbook that has songs in twenty-three languages. There was a very cool Israeli dance team helping lead worship. They had Israeli costumes and some great choreography. Afterwards there was a blowing of seven trumpets. Tom, who was the main organizer of the convocation, welcomed us and spoke of the significance of Israel in the fulfilling of God's purposes in these last days. There was such an air of energy and expectancy about why we had gathered and looking at what God might do. Looking forward to tomorrow.

Tuesday–
Went up to the lobby to find Greg and company. They had left for the old city. A fellow I'd met the first night from Timbuktu, Mali, was there. He had some trade beads from Africa in his room that he wanted to show me. So we went to his room. He dresses in his traditional many-layered robe every day. He sat on the floor and I pulled up a small ottoman as he opened up his suitcase. Inside each bag were a variety of different beads, necklaces and stones. Many he said were several hundred years old. As he was showing me these things he shared his personal story with me. He comes from a Muslim family in Mali. When he became a Christian, his family disowned him. Many of the believers here are from Muslim countries. To serve Jesus is a great sacrifice for many. Bought a really cool knife from him for Ian for his birthday and several smaller knives for the other boys. Good meetings this evening. Called home tonight, good hearing everyone. Couldn't believe Daniel broke his wrist. Boys!

Wednesday–
Before breakfast we begin meeting at 7.00 each morning. We have ten to fifteen minutes of worship which is never enough. It's like a high-spirited horse, always wanting to take his rein and break into a full gallop. The rider is always saying, 'whoa, easy now'. You might imagine with these 'world class' intercessory types and national prayer leaders that we could just go soaring in worship forever. But even the few minutes we have is rich. Then we have a teaching on some aspect of the prophetic.

We go to breakfast till 9.00 and then gather back together for ten to fifteen minutes of worship, then hear reports from the nations of the world. Each country is given five to seven minutes to share how to pray for their nation. I've learned so much about the different countries and their histories. It's been pretty amazing to see the way God is moving among the nations. We heard from brothers from North Africa today. An older pastor had come from Cairo, Egypt. It's a heavy scene to be a Christian in Egypt. We also heard from one of the leaders in the Coptic Church of Egypt. The Coptics are like a Greek Orthodox-flavor of Christianity.

We then pray together for each country one at a time after each national representative gives their report. Today, a Bahamian friend I met in Korea, and Jim and I walked to the old city. From our hotel we are across the way from Mt. Zion and the old city of Jerusalem. We had a good day just being together. I bought a few things in the markets. Such an interesting place, the market. An old Bedouin was on the streets with this huge tea pot apparatus strapped on his back. The top was filled with a bunch of little bells and cymbals to make noise. He has paper cups and when you order one he bends forward to fill your cup from the spout which sticks out from above his shoulder. It was a sweet coffee/tea-like cold drink. I bought a necklace from a guy. (Most shop owners are hard-core, heavily aggressive fellows). This guy, he says, 'I love you Indian, but if you buy from me I will love you more'. We started at $53.00 and ended up at $20.00. He was even upset that I bought it for $20.00. The next day he said, 'Hey Indian, you are the one who broke my heart!'

This other guy was selling these large pictures of the old city of Jerusalem for 10 shekels (3 shekels = $1.00). I told him I'd buy two for ten. He said eighteen. I said ten. He said OK, fifteen. I said ten. He said fourteen. I said, OK, I'll buy two for twelve. He said no. So I started to walk away and he said OK. This is how it goes.

We walked back to the hotel at about 5.00. Tonight was our night to share from the USA. I didn't have a chance on the plane ride to sew on the horsehair pieces [some tribes commonly sew tufts of horsehair on their regalia], so I spent an hour sewing. As I was dressing in my regalia, many came and 'oohed' and 'aahed'. All the hotel staff men came and talked to me. They asked all kinds of questions about Indians. One guy did his best to talk me out of an eagle feather. When I walked into the meeting area half the people stood and clapped and 'oohed' and 'aahed'. I was pretty good about sticking to my seven-minute limit. I shared about Native people generally and my dream for world evangelization and then I led in a prayer of repentance for Native people. Jim, Greg, and I held the flag together during the prayer time. Many wept out loud and there was a time of real intercession for Native people. Afterward, many people said lots of encouraging words to Greg and me.

After the meeting, 'Bill', the worship leader and his cohort 'Dave', who are both Jewish, invited Greg and me out to dinner. After driving around this part of the city we ended up at a very nice Chinese restaurant. Bill, who was an old hippie musician in Detroit growing up with Motown and rhythm and blues, got saved in the Jesus Movement. He had been pastoring a national messianic Jewish congregation with his wife in Jerusalem for the past eight years. He told some very far-out stories about being in the Israeli Army. He has been on border patrol for months at a time where the Syrian and Lebanese borders intersect with Israel. He talked of how the Bedouin men serve as incredible trackers for the army. As people of the desert, they know the ways of the land in an almost mystical way. Finally hit the hay about 1.15 a.m.

Thursday–
Woke up a little late and got down to the meeting about thirty minutes late. Again was good. Sat with a really sweet brother from Serbia. Invited me and the family over anytime. Good time of worship after breakfast – a couple from France have been leading worship when Bill doesn't. We heard from Eastern Europe. Estonia, Lithuania, Poland, Bulgaria, Albania, Hungary, Czechoslovakia, Slovakia, Croatia, Bosnia, Serbia, Latvia, and Macedonia. Some heavy stories of human suffering and tragedy in these countries. We also heard from all the Scandinavian countries. A neat guy is here from the Farroe Islands. Never heard of the place actually. It's an island country between Norway and Iceland. It's interesting that all of their national flags have the cross as the singular design – just different colors and positioning. They have Christian heritages?

Afterwards, Greg and I went to the new city to find a bank and get some bucks. After much wandering around, we found a bank only to discover I needed my passport to use my Visa card.

That evening, we heard from Western Europe. Came in when Great Britain was up. Heard from England, Wales, Scotland, Northern and southern Ireland. Lots of repentance on the part of England. As much as England was a blessing to the world, it also subjected much of the world to bondage and a colonial spirit. This was and is a curse now in their nations. The most moving experience for me thus far was listening to the brother from Northern Ireland. The pain in his heart for his people was very powerful. So much pain and suffering in Ireland. Many of us wept with our brother as he sobbed and sobbed. And the other lady from the Republic of Ireland shared how in the tenth or twelfth centuries, somewhere in there, that Ireland, under the leadership of St. Patrick, was the country that evangelized Europe. There was much repentance on their parts. We had a very powerful time of prayer on their behalf.

Afterward, Greg and I, Jim, and our friend from Samoa, had a piece of pie together. These things, prayer conferences, are always such a blessing. Meeting new guys and hanging out with the fellows is very special. All the jokes and funny stories are wonderful. Got back to the room about 11.30. An early night. Each night Jim or I talk a little about our families and what we're involved in. I leave tomorrow so I've packed up one of my bags so I'm at least half way done because we are taking off tomorrow for the Sea of Galilee.

Saturday–

Since I shared Wednesday night, many people have come up to me and thanked me for my words. Probably the biggest part of why people's hearts were so moved is because they didn't know any Christian (or even if there were any at all) Native Americans. That fact in itself has been a cause of real joy for many.

I know there is a growing anointing in my life to speak these things, but I have been struck with a sense of wonderment about how God is going to be using me and Kath [Twiss] in the days ahead. I somehow have felt enlarged or expanded in my spirit since being here. The thought that 'the stakes have gotten bigger' has been recurring in my thoughts. It would seem that in recent months with meeting Jim, IBS [International Bible Society], and with the NANCC [North American Native Christian Council] conference soon to happen, the ante for me has definitely risen. So many opportunities. Many here said they would welcome a team of Native dancers to their countries and arrange meetings, etc. Jim said he would help raise money for a team to go overseas. I don't know where it will eventually lead. And in the very middle of all this is how Kath and I and the boys fit together. With the boys growing older, the stakes are definitely going up.

Woke up early this morning to be picked up at 5.00 a.m. at the hotel. Greg and Jim also woke with me and we stood on the roof of the hotel, which is actually street level, and prayed together and watched the sun come up over Jerusalem. I was told I should be at the airport 2 ½ to 3 hours early. It was Shabbat and very early so there were few cars on the road, allowing us to make a very speedy trip to Tel Aviv Airport. A little apprehensive after our Portland episode, but my driver assures me it should be no problem.

The Israeli airport security personnel, this morning at least, are all in their early and mid-twenties. The first one asked me a ton of questions and then a second asked me another ton, many the same. Took about twenty minutes. After clearing customs, I bought a few last-minute items in the duty-free stores. Sitting on the plane and ready to go, I was prepared for a long nine to ten-hour flight only to find out going west you fly against the winds so it'll be an eleven or twelve - hour flight. Oh joy.

Been thinking how I could've used about three or four more days. It was difficult getting in the groove of the convocation. Felt I was just starting to get grooved in. Especially in relationships with people.

Made it to New York and now am flying home to Portland via a forty-five-minute stop in Seattle. Will have been up twenty hours by the time I get home. All on only five hours of sleep the night before.

FOLLOWING CREATOR'S SON JESUS

My adventure with Creator's son Jesus began when I invited him into my life as a nine-year-old. There was a time as an adult when I walked away from him, but he never walked away from me. When I came to my senses, I realized that asking Jesus into my heart as savior didn't mean I had asked him to be 'in charge' of my life – *to be my Lord*. I made that choice as an adult.

Three years after becoming 'born again', I was baptized in the Holy Spirit.

Jesus didn't come to earth just to give us good rules to follow, although following good rules is beneficial. He came primarily to restore our relationship with the Father. Jesus came to give us life, and that abundantly (Jn 10.10).

Jeremiah 1.5 says, 'Before I formed you in the womb I knew you, before you were born I set you apart. I appointed you as a prophet to the nations'. I believe that God has an extraordinary plan for each of us, just as he did for Jeremiah, but we must choose to follow that plan.

If you have not yet met Creator's son Jesus, we invite you to ask him into your heart. Holy Spirit enters your heart when you make that decision. We also encourage you to then seek the anointing (baptism) of the Holy Spirit to activate the power, the fire, and the gifts of the Spirit listed in 1 Cor. 12.1-11.

God never changes – he is still looking for those he can prove himself powerful to, 'to show Himself strong on behalf of *those* whose heart *is* loyal to Him' (2 Chron. 16.9). Allow him to enter your heart, change it, *and* change the world through you!

Sue Martell
August 2017

BIBLIOGRAPHY

Church, Casey, *Holy Smoke: The Contextual Use of Native American Ritual and Ceremony* (ed. Ray Martell and Sue Martell; Cleveland, TN: Cherohala Press, 2017).

Eastman, Charles Alexander (Ohiyesa), *The Soul of an Indian and Other Writings from Ohiyesa* (ed. Kent Nerburn; Novato, CA: New World Library, 2001).

Fonseca, Felicia, 'Author Convicted in Ariz. Sweat Lodge Deaths Freed', www.nbcnews.com/news/other/author-convicted-ariz-sweat-lodge-deaths-freed-f6C10620484. July 12, 2013. Accessed May 4, 2017.

Indigenous Pathways, https://indigenouspathways.com/aboutIP.html. Accessed Oct. 28, 2016.

NAIITS: An Indigenous Learning Community, http://www.naiits.com/history/. Accessed Mar. 20, 2017.

National Congress of American Indians, 'Indian Nations in the United States', http://www.ncai.org/about-tribes/indians_101.pdf. Accessed Nov. 20, 2016.

Pratt, Richard H., 'The Advantages of Mingling Indians with Whites', in F.P. Prucha (ed.), *Americanizing the American Indians: Writings by the 'Friends of the Indian,' 1880-1900* (Cambridge, MA: Harvard University Press, 1973), pp. 46-59.

Rich, Tracey, 'Judaism 101', http://www.jewfaq.org/index.shtml. Accessed Oct. 27, 2016.

Suuqiina, Qaumaniq and Iglahliq Suuqiina, *Warfare by Honor: The Restoration of Honor: A Protocol Handbook* (Scotland, PA: Healing the Land Publishing, 2007).

Twiss, Richard, *Rescuing the Gospel from the Cowboys: A Native American Expression of the Jesus Way* (ed. Ray Martell and Sue Martell; Downers Grove, IL: InterVarsity Press, 2015).

—'Three Past and Three Future: Leadership from Dr. Richard Twiss' (presentation at the Beyond Colorblind 2013 conference at Gordon College, 2013). https://youtu.be/IkjSA6x UHms, Accessed Apr. 30, 2017.

—'Salmon Nation Handbook', www.wiconi.com, 2011.

—'Making Jesus Known in Knowable Ways', *Mission Frontiers* (September-October, 2010). http://www.missionfrontiers.org/issue/article/making-jesus-known-in-knowable-ways. Accessed October 27, 2016.

—*One Church, Many Tribes: Following Jesus the Way God Made You* (Ventura, CA: Regal Books, 2000).

Woodley, Randy, *Shalom and the Community of Creation: An Indigenous Vision* (Grand Rapids, MI: Eerdmans Publishing Company, 2012).

—*Living in Color: Embracing God's Passion for Ethnic Diversity* (Downers Grove, IL: InterVarsity Press, 2004).

—*Mixed Blood, Not Mixed Up: Finding God-given Identity in a Multi-cultural World* (Scotland, PA: Healing the Land Publishing, 2005).

INDEX OF BIBLICAL REFERENCES

Exodus
30.34-36   76

Leviticus
23.40   75

Numbers
22.30   74

Joshua
1.8   74
10.12   75

Deuteronomy
7.9   101

2 Chronicles
16.9   115

Job
1.10   95

Psalms
139.3, 13-16   64
145.4   69

Isaiah
6.8   3
49.16   95

Jeremiah
1.4-5   1
1.5   115

Ezekiel
1.10-11   76
37.9   75

Matthew
7.17-18   92

Mark
4.39   74

11.22-25   74

John
5.19   15
10.10   115
17.20-21   100

Acts
17.6   1

Romans
8.28   1
10.15   66
12.2   77

1 Corinthians
9.22   53
12.1-11   115

1 Peter
2.9   97

INDEX OF NAMES

Blake, M.   79
Brown, D.   78
Church, C.   11, 13, 14, 65, 75, 82, 86, 87, 89, 90
Eastman, C.   83
Fonseca, F.   88
Jacobs, A.   33, 64
Nerburn, K.   83.

Pratt, R.   72
Rich, T.   75
Suuqiina, Q. and I.   86
Twiss, R.   8, 12, 14, 15, 19, 20, 25, 26, 28-30, 32, 34-36, 38-40, 42, 43, 45-47, 49-52, 58, 71, 77-79, 82, 84, 87, 92, 97, 99, 102-106
Woodley, R.   10, 64, 75, 79

ABOUT THE AUTHORS

Sue Martell is a Registered Nurse who has worked in ministry for more than ten years as the Nurse Manager of a Christian pro-life pregnancy clinic. She has a Bachelor of Science degree in Nursing and a Master of Public Administration.

Ray has a Bachelor of Arts in English Literature and a Master of Adult and Continuing Education. He previously worked as a community college teacher, broadcast journalist, editor of Air Force newspapers, and public affairs officer. He's been working for a local library system for the past fifteen years.

Sue and Ray are both USAF veterans. Sue was in the Nurse Corps and Ray served in Operations Desert Shield and Storm. He was on General Schwarzkopf's staff as a media relations officer.

Sue and Ray have worked together in Native American contextual ministry as volunteers for both Wiconi and NAIITS: An Indigenous Learning Community (formerly the North American Institute for Indigenous Theological Studies) for more than eight years.

Together, Ray and Sue edited the late Dr Richard Twiss's *Rescuing the Gospel from the Cowboys: A Native American Expression of the Jesus Way.* They edited Dr Casey Church's *Holy Smoke: The Contextual Use of Native American Ritual and Ceremony,* and authored its foreword.

Sue and Ray live on a beautiful island in the Pacific Northwest. They have two adult children.

MINISTRY RESOURCES:

Indigenous Pathways is a non-profit organization which includes the following ministries:

Wiconi: (contextual cultural celebration) wiconi.com

NAIITS: (an indigenous learning community) naiits.com

iEmergence: (contextual ministry in the Philippines) iemergence.org
My People: (First Nations Canada contextual ministry) mypeople-international.com

---

Mending Wings: (contextual youth ministry) mendingwings.net

Eagles Wings Ministry/Eloheh: (Eloheh farm, school and mentoring) eagleswingsministry.com

Carry the Cure (suicide prevention ministry): carrythecure.org

Polished Arrow: (First Nations directory and resources) polishedarrow.com

42896148R00077

Made in the USA
Middletown, DE
18 April 2019